Current
CONTROVERSIES

The Iranian
Green Movement

Other Books in the Current Controversies Series

The Iranian
Green Movement

Debra A. Miller, Book Editor

GREENHAVEN PRESS
A part of Gale, Cengage Learning

Detroit • New York • San Francisco • New Haven, Conn • Waterville, Maine • London

Elizabeth Des Chenes, *Managing Editor*

© 2012 Greenhaven Press, a part of Gale, Cengage Learning

Gale and Greenhaven Press are registered trademarks used herein under license.

For more information, contact:
Greenhaven Press
27500 Drake Rd.
Farmington Hills, MI 48331-3535
Or you can visit our Internet site at gale.cengage.com

LIBRARY OF CONGRESS CATALOGING-IN-PUBLICATION DATA

The Iranian green movement / Debra A. Miller, book editor.
   p. cm. -- (Current controversies)
   Includes bibliographical references and index.
   ISBN 978-0-7377-5626-5 (hardcover) -- ISBN 978-0-7377-5627-2 (pbk.)
   1. Green movement--Iran. 2. Environmentalism--Iran. 3. Iran--Politics and government. 4. Iran--Environmental conditions. I. Miller, Debra A.
   GE199.I7I73 2012
   333.720955--dc23
                                                          2011024263

Printed in the United States of America
1 2 3 4 5   15 14 13 12 11

FD319

Contents

Chapter 1: What Is the Nature of Iran's Green Movement?

Austin Bay

Although economic issues and government repression are also involved, the Iranian protests began because of government corruption; namely, election fraud during the June 12, 2009, presidential election. Iran's leaders now face what could be a sustained struggle with a new generation of Iranians who were not part of the 1979 Islamic Revolution.

Mahmood Delkhasteh, interviewed
by Behdad Bordbar

Iranian protesters have demanded freedom, democracy, and respect for human rights; however, Iran's constitution gives an unelected supreme leader absolute power over all aspects of society and government—a system that cannot implement the protesters' demands. The green movement is thus revolutionary because it can only achieve its goals by removing the current regime and changing Iran's system of government.

Arshin Adib-Moghaddam

The protests in Iran are not a revolt against Iran's Islamic Republic system of government but rather just a renegotiation of power in a postrevolutionary nation. The Islamic Revolution of 1979 achieved independence and created an Islamic Republic, and now the green movement demands a third goal—freedom from government oppression.

Chapter 2: Has Iran's Green Movement Been Destroyed?

Many commentators criticize US President Barack Obama's response to Iran's green movement and argue that a more forceful US response could have helped the revolution succeed; however, the movement never really had a chance at overthrowing the Iranian regime because the regime still has significant support in rural areas of the country and among more religious Iranians.

No: Iran's Green Movement Has Not Been Destroyed

Chapter 3: Is Iran's Green Movement Related to Uprisings in Tunisia and Egypt?

Foreword

By definition, controversies are "discussions of questions in which opposing opinions clash" (*Webster's Twentieth Century Dictionary Unabridged*). Few would deny that controversies are a pervasive part of the human condition and exist on virtually every level of human enterprise. Controversies transpire between individuals and among groups, within nations and between nations. Controversies supply the grist necessary for progress by providing challenges and challengers to the status quo. They also create atmospheres where strife and warfare can flourish. A world without controversies would be a peaceful world; but it also would be, by and large, static and prosaic.

The Series' Purpose

The purpose of the Current Controversies series is to explore many of the social, political, and economic controversies dominating the national and international scenes today. Titles selected for inclusion in the series are highly focused and specific. For example, from the larger category of criminal justice, Current Controversies deals with specific topics such as police brutality, gun control, white collar crime, and others. The debates in Current Controversies also are presented in a useful, timeless fashion. Articles and book excerpts included in each title are selected if they contribute valuable, long-range ideas to the overall debate. And wherever possible, current information is enhanced with historical documents and other relevant materials. Thus, while individual titles are current in focus, every effort is made to ensure that they will not become quickly outdated. Books in the Current Controversies series will remain important resources for librarians, teachers, and students for many years.

In addition to keeping the titles focused and specific, great care is taken in the editorial format of each book in the series. Book introductions and chapter prefaces are offered to provide background material for readers. Chapters are organized around several key questions that are answered with diverse opinions representing all points on the political spectrum. Materials in each chapter include opinions in which authors clearly disagree as well as alternative opinions in which authors may agree on a broader issue but disagree on the possible solutions. In this way, the content of each volume in Current Controversies mirrors the mosaic of opinions encountered in society. Readers will quickly realize that there are many viable answers to these complex issues. By questioning each author's conclusions, students and casual readers can begin to develop the critical thinking skills so important to evaluating opinionated material.

Current Controversies is also ideal for controlled research. Each anthology in the series is composed of primary sources taken from a wide gamut of informational categories including periodicals, newspapers, books, US and foreign government documents, and the publications of private and public organizations. Readers will find factual support for reports, debates, and research papers covering all areas of important issues. In addition, an annotated table of contents, an index, a book and periodical bibliography, and a list of organizations to contact are included in each book to expedite further research.

Perhaps more than ever before in history, people are confronted with diverse and contradictory information. During the Persian Gulf War, for example, the public was not only treated to minute-to-minute coverage of the war, it was also inundated with critiques of the coverage and countless analyses of the factors motivating US involvement. Being able to sort through the plethora of opinions accompanying today's major issues, and to draw one's own conclusions, can be a complicated and frustrating struggle. It is the editors' hope that Current Controversies will help readers with this struggle.

Introduction

"*Many of today's Iranian protesters view the 1979 Islamic revolution as the creator of yet another autocratic regime—this one ruled by religious clerics who have been willing to use force against fellow Iranians to hold on to power.*"

Many young Iranians participated in protests in 2009 and 2010 aimed at reforming or toppling Iran's ruling regime, but the country's current government system was created just a few decades ago in an earlier popular revolt—the 1979 Islamic revolution. The 1979 revolution, according to most experts, was a reaction to a long-lived monarchy that modernized the country but suppressed Iranians' desires for democracy as well as the power of Islamic religious leaders. Ironically, many of today's Iranian protesters view the 1979 Islamic revolution as the creator of yet another autocratic regime—this one ruled by religious clerics who have been willing to use force against fellow Iranians to hold on to power.

Prior to the 1979 revolution, Iran was ruled by Mohammad Reza Shah, a shah, or king, that the United States and Great Britain helped to install in a 1953 coup. The main motive for the coup was to allow Britain to gain control over Iran's oil fields, which Iran nationalized in 1951 under the leadership of Mohammad Mossadeq, who later was elected as Iran's prime minister. The 1953 coup ousted Mossadeq in order to place a pro-Western monarch in power, ensuring the British continuing access to Iranian oil. Another reason for the coup was US and British fear of communism following World War II; installing a new king backed by Western powers helped to squelch a fledgling Communist Party that had taken root in Iran. Many Iranians, however, viewed the 1953 coup as an unacceptable and heavy-handed foreign intervention in Iran's affairs, and it planted a bitter seed of anti-Americanism in Iran that lingers to the present day.

For the next twenty-six years after the coup, the shah ruled Iran with an iron fist, ignoring Iran's constitution, which limited royal powers and provided for a representative government, and using secret police and the Iranian army to suppress any challenge to his government. The shah also established close relations with the United States and other Western nations—relationships that further strengthened his political base and made Iran a regional power. At the same time, the shah promoted reforms that grew Iran's economy, expanded education, empowered women, and decreased the power of religious elites. Many Iranians benefited from the shah's policies, but the policies also angered both students and intellectuals who sought democratic reforms and religious leaders who felt that they were being marginalized in an increasingly secular, Westernized society.

By the mid-1970s, the discontent with the shah's rule had grown significantly, and exiled Islamic leader Ayatollah Ruhollah Khomeini began calling for the overthrow of the shah. In 1978, mass protests spread throughout the country, spurred on by pro-Khomeini cassette tapes that were smuggled into Iran by supporters. On January 16, 1979, the shah fled Iran, leaving a new prime minister and the army in charge. Ayatollah Khomeini returned to Iran shortly thereafter, and in April 1979, he declared Iran to be an Islamic Republic with a new constitution. The new government was approved by a large majority of Iranians in a referendum election. Voters replaced Iran's secular government with a theocracy ruled by religious leaders called mullahs, although Iran also elects a president and legislature to run the country under the mullahs' direction. In November 1979, Iranians also took out their frustrations on America, when young Khomeini supporters attacked the US embassy and took dozens of Americans hostage.

The American hostages were eventually released in January 1981, but the event signaled the establishment of a new, radicalized, anti-American Iran. Khomeini openly proclaimed the United States to be an enemy of Islam, calling America the Great Satan. After Khomeini's death in 1989, Iran's leaders continued this anti-American posture and extended it to America's ally, Israel. Iran also sought to export its Islamic fundamentalism by supporting Hezbollah, an Islamic militant group in Lebanon that the United States considers to be a terrorist organization. In addition, Iran went to war with neighboring Iraq in the 1980s, and after the United States toppled the Iraqi regime of Saddam Hussein in 2003, Iran has sought to gain influence there. In recent years, many experts believe that Iran has embarked on a course aimed at developing nuclear weapons, in order to make Iran a nuclear power in the Middle East—a prospect feared by neighboring states like Israel.

Iran's Islamic leaders also imposed radical policies within Iran. Although the Islamic revolution originally had many supporters, it ultimately created a government as repressive as the shah's regime. Iran does hold elections, but religious leaders control the military and judiciary, determine who is allowed to run for president, set the nation's policies, and approve all legislation. In the name of Islam, many new restrictions were placed on women's dress and behavior, requiring them to cover their heads and wear full-body cloaks and limiting their rights of inheritance and other basic freedoms. Western music and culture were banned, and the press is monitored closely by the government. In addition, political protests are quickly met with lethal force, and tens of thousands of political activists have been imprisoned or executed over the years.

Despite these restrictions, a strong undercurrent of resistance to Iran's Islamic regime has developed within Iran. It was dramatically revealed in 2009, when thousands of mostly young Iranians turned out to protest the results of the country's 2009 presidential elections. The official election results showed that incumbent president Mahmoud Ahmadinejad had won, but there were allegations of voting irregularities, and protesters believed that their candidate, Mir-Hossein Mousavi, should have won. The protests continued for several months, but the regime responded with a violent crackdown, arrests of protest leaders and their relatives, and a ban on future demonstrations.

Iran's reform movement, often called the green movement because protesters adopted Mousavi's campaign color as their signature symbol, is the subject of *Current Controversies: The Iranian Green Movement*. Authors of viewpoints in this volume present a range of views about the nature of the green movement, whether it has been destroyed, whether it is related to the string of antigovernment protests in other parts of the Middle East, and the prospects for the movement's future.

CHAPTER 1

What Is the Nature of Iran's Green Movement?

Chapter Preface

Shortly after protests broke out following the June 12, 2009, elections in Iran, the Iranian reform movement—often called the green movement because of its signature color—had its first martyr. In the early evening of June 20, 2009, Neda Agha-Soltan, a twenty-six-year-old aspiring singer and student from a middle-class Iranian family, was shot and killed by Iranian police as she stood at the edge of protests in Tehran, Iran's capital city. Remarkably, her last moments were captured on video by bystanders and the videos were posted on the Internet, allowing millions of people around the world to watch in shock as her lifeblood streamed from her nose and mouth. Overnight, Neda became an international symbol of the brutality of the Iranian government, and her name was invoked by world leaders including US president Barack Obama. She was hailed as a martyr for the green movement. But Neda was not the first to die at the hands of Iranian security enforcers, nor the last; since 2009, Iran's governing regime has used mass and selected arrests, detention, imprisonment, and executions and other forms of lethal force to prevent street protests and suppress the reform movement.

The green movement developed as a protest against alleged election fraud in the June 2009, Iranian presidential elections. Incumbent Iranian president Mahmoud Ahmadinejad was pitted against a pro-reform candidate, Mir-Hossein Mousavi, who became the favorite of many young, pro-democracy Iranians. Polls taken before the election were mixed, with many showing Ahmadinejad in the lead, and a few suggesting that Mousavi was ahead. The official election results, however, showed Ahmadinejad as the clear winner, with 63 percent of the vote compared with 34 percent garnered by Mousavi. News sources in some Western nations questioned the results, and some observers inside Iran claimed that there were irregularities in the voting, such as stuffed ballot boxes and people voting without identification. Mousavi publicly disputed the result, and he urged his supporters to peacefully resist. The morning after the election, protesters turned out in Tehran contesting the election and claiming it was fraudulent.

Protests grew over the next few days, and the movement became known as the green movement, because that color was used by Mousavi in his presidential campaign and was displayed by many of the protesters. After an official appeal by Mousavi, Iran's supreme leader, Ayatollah Ali Khamenei responded by announcing there would be an investigation, but a June 29 recount announcement confirmed Ahmadinejad as the winner. Protesters responded to this news with even larger demonstrations and with repeated clashes with Iranian police, producing a number of protester injuries and deaths. Some protesters called for the overthrow of the Iranian government, chanting slogans such as "Death to the Dictator."

It was the shooting of Agha-Soltan on June 20, 2009, however, and the video showing her last dying breaths that galvanized Iranian and international attention for the protest movement. At about 6:30 in the evening, as Neda stood watching the protests with her music teacher, witnesses saw a member of the Basij, a government militia group, take aim and shoot Neda in the chest. She collapsed to the ground and was attended by a doctor who happened to be in the crowd. Bystanders recorded the next seventy seconds on video, as Neda's eyes rolled to the right, she appeared to lose consciousness, and blood streamed from her mouth and nose. The video energized the protests, which continued throughout the next several months.

The Iranian government, however, has steadfastly denied responsibility for Neda's death, and the regime ultimately succeeded in crushing the demonstrations. The regime evicted foreign journalists and conducted mass arrests, detentions without trial, and violence against protesters, including numerous beatings and killings. Security police also stormed the homes of leading dissidents, clerics, and activists, making arrests and issuing threats against their families. Many of those arrested were thrown into Iran's notorious prisons, which are known to use various forms of torture against prisoners. In the months following the initial crackdown, according to human rights experts, the Iranian government has also detained Mousavi under house arrest, forced imprisoned dissidents to make false confessions, and conducted show trials of leading political figures who were seen as sympathetic to the reform movement. Always a leading nation in the number of executions it performs annually, Iran has recently increased this pattern, executing close to a hundred prisoners just in the first month of 2011.

With the Iranian government back in control and the green movement now in the shadows, various commentators have sought to analyze the movement's goals and tactics. The authors of the viewpoints in this chapter debate issues such as the role of social-networking media and whether the movement seeks to achieve election reforms, an expansion of civil rights, or a complete overthrow of the Islamic regime.

The Iranian Green Movement Is a Protest Against Government Corruption

Austin Bay

Austin Bay is an author, syndicated columnist, and professor, as well as a war game designer and principal in a training simulations and technology consulting company.

Economic misery and repression played roles, but an overt act of corruption brought the people into the streets.

One year ago [in June 2009], election fraud ignited demonstrations throughout Iran. Stealing the national election held on June 12, 2009, was one theft too many by the religious dictatorship and its cronies.

Established by the Ayatollah Ruhollah Khomeini in 1979, Iran's radical cleric-controlled regime ("mullocracy" is the pop term [meaning "rule by mullahs," the Muslim clerics]) came to power deploring the Shah's [Iran's former king] theft and corruption. Khomeinist Islamic revolutionary values would ensure two things: 1) a harsh, but clean Iranian national government and 2) the spread of Khomeinist-led Islamic revolution around the world by any means necessary, including successful political example, economic might, subterfuge, terrorism, guerrillas and, when necessary, all-out war.

Islamic Revolution Failures

The mullahs' attempts to fulfill their second revolutionary pledge to extend Khomeini's revolution beyond Iran's borders, however, have been destructive but largely unsuccessful. Decades of political finagling and terrorist activities in the Persian Gulf have not toppled a single Arab government.

Iran's attempts to use proxies to destroy Iraq's nascent democratic government have left thousands dead and slowed Iraqi development, but "the Arabs" continue to build a new society in Mesopotamia [the ancient name for Iraq]. Afghanistan, the bloody puzzle to the east, has NATO [North Atlantic Treaty Organization, an alliance of European nations and the USA] troops. Global revolution has left Iran in a strategic vise. A nuclear weapon, however, might change that.

Stealing the national election held on June 12, 2009, was one theft too many by the religious dictatorship and its cronies.

The regime's failure to keep the revolution's first pledge, the promise the Khomeinists used to ignite popular revolt against the Shah, however, has divided Iran's people and created what is ultimately a more potent and dangerous threat to the mullahs than American or Israeli bombs. Harsh domestic government the revolution provided, but as for clean?

While Khomeini lived, the crooks kept up the pretense of spic and span—maybe. Khomeini died in 1989. Economic decline in Iran, tied to mismanagement and corruption, was evident by the early 1990s, when the first serious calls for systemic reform began.

The complaints received lip service. Reformers, like Ayatollah Mohamed Khatami (who was elected president in 1997), were isolated politically and rendered powerless. Subsequently, the Khomeinist regime rigged the voting system to exclude future Khatami-type intruders.

The situation faced by most Iranians deteriorated. A telling conversation took place some six years ago when a knowledgeable Iranian told me the total bribe required for permission to acquire land and launch a major construction project in Tehran [Iran's capital] had gone from $50,000 or so to around a half million—in American dollars, please.

Another source asserted the Shia [a Muslim sect] clerics running Iran were more aggressive thieves than the Palavis, the Shah's despised clan. Call it old gossip—perhaps CIA [US Central Intelligence Agency] knows the precise Tehran bribe schedule circa 2004—but new gossip says the corruption has gotten worse.

The cultural straightjacket of clerical puritanism chafes youths who want to rock and roll, and the mullahs' blatant hypocrisy and corruption adds to their [the youths'] disenchantment and alienation.

A Divided Nation

Public demonstrations and anti-regime declarations—verifiable facts—show Iran enters the 21st century's second decade a profoundly divided nation. Time is a threat to all revolutions. As years pass, the revolutionaries age and the fervor fades. A generational divide often emerges, and it has in Iran.

The Green Movement, the umbrella anti-government grouping that emerged from the post-election demonstrations in 2009, has a large following among Iran's youth and middle-aged.

Most Iranians under the age of 40 have little truck with the ruling mullahs. The Shah is ancient history. The Council of Guardians' [a part of Iran's government] cruelty is current news. The cultural straightjacket of clerical puritanism chafes youths who want to rock and roll, and the mullahs' blatant hypocrisy and corruption adds to their [the youths'] disenchantment and alienation.

The mullahs know domestically they face a sustained, popular struggle against their endemically corrupt regime. The Green Movement, however, is a hodgepodge of factions, including reformists (who support extensive, rapid reform), incrementalists (who favor certain reforms) and radicals of all sorts (some promoting Western-style democracy).

The mullahs and the Revolutionary Guards exploit these divisions. Their policy of jailing movement leaders, threatening family members and selectively repressing Green Movement factions has kept the Green Movement from coalescing as a genuine revolutionary organization. So far.

The Iranian Green Movement Is Revolutionary

Mahmood Delkhasteh, interviewed by Behdad Bordbar

Mahmood Delkhasteh is an Iranian scholar and commentator. Behdad Bordbar is a journalist working with Radio Zamaneh, an Amsterdam, Holland–based Persian language radio station.

June 12 [2010] was the first anniversary of Iran's tenth presidential election. I had a chance to discuss the development and challenges of the Green movement with Dr Mahmood Delkhasteh.

[Behdad Bordbar:] In its contemporary history, Iran experienced three major social movements: the Constitutional Revolution (1905–1911), the oil nationalization movement (1951–1953) and the Islamic Revolution (1979). Despite this, we have been unable to establish democracy. What makes the Green movement different?

[Mahmood Delkhasteh:] It is true that although the goal of all three movements was to establish freedom and independence, all failed to achieve this. Upon closer look, however, each of these apparent failures has brought us closer to establishing democracy. Despotism in Iran has historically had three interrelated internal bases: economic (big landownership in the rural economy and the bazaar [open marketplace] in urban life), political (the monarchy) and cultural (the clergy). The Shah [Iran's former king] had to abolish big landownership in the 1960s, which, in combination with the weakening of oil income and the import economy, also drastically weakened the bazaar. The monarchy was abolished in the 1979 revolution. After this, the re-emergence of dictatorship was based only on its cultural base, the clergy, which made it fragile. In order to overcome this fragility, the regime implemented a policy of crisis making (the current one being, of course, nuclear). During the presidency of [Mahmoud] Ahmadinejad, the revolutionary guards have gradually either pushed the clergy away or deserted them. The ruling regime is the most fragile the country has ever experienced.

[Iran's] ruling military-financial mafia has nothing to offer to the young but threats and violence.

The Green movement emerged within this context, which is why the regime has relied so much on brute force. It lacks virtually any legitimacy. Now we have a government, built on a rigged election, which is thus completely paralyzed. Except from signing the agreement with Turkey and Brazil in regard to the nuclear issue, Iran has not been able to carry out any serious policy. The Green movement therefore has a greater chance of establishing democracy than ever before.

However, unlike other revolutions, it suffers from a lack of visionary and decisive leadership. In other words, the leadership of the Green movement is its Achilles heel. Their aim is not to establish a democracy, but a limited form of freedom, through implementing the constitution, in which the leader has total authority over state and society. The majority of the public want to see the end of this regime, while their leaders have remained fiercely reformist. This is the main reason for the weakening of the movement.

Despite the brutal oppression by authorities, what makes you optimistic about the future of the movement?

I am optimistic because the ruling military-financial mafia has nothing to offer to the young but threats and violence. Their sheer ineptitude and widespread corruption at every level of state and government has made it impossible to seek, let alone implement, long-term solutions. Take the Tiananmen square massacre [in Beijing, China, in 1989] in comparison. The Chinese government was determined not to relinquish political power, but offered [protesters] economic progress and prosperity. As a result, China has emerged as a global economic power. Even this is not possible in Iran, due to the nature and organization of the regime. So young people are faced with a stark choice of watching their hopes for the future collapse at the bloody hands of a thoroughly corrupt regime, or replacing it with a democratic government. There are no other choices. The history of the last hundred years tells us that whenever Iranians have been faced with such a decision, they have chosen life and freedom over slow death under despotism.

However, my optimism is not permanent or absolute. This is because power never dissolves itself; it has to be dissolved again and again. In order to accomplish this, the Iranian people should abandon the vain hope of reforming this system. It is only in the death of such naive hope that revolutionary hope will be born. Unfortunately, reformist intellectuals have managed to equate the idea of revolution with violence and despotism, and reform with non-violence and democracy. This has created a climate of fear amongst the young, who are afraid to bring this movement to its logical conclusion. As long as this politics of fear dominates the understanding of revolution, the movement cannot become widespread.

How do you characterize this movement? Do you think it is a reformist project, a civil rights movement or a revolutionary struggle?

To define a movement, we have to understand its demands within the context in which it takes place. What is being demanded of what? In this approach, situating the guiding principles as stated in demonstrations against the status quo, the Green movement can only be considered revolutionary. Contrast it, for example, to the American Civil Rights Movement.

When Martin Luther King, Jr. waged his crusade for racial equality, he justified his demands by referring to the US Declaration of Independence, which established a foundational principle that all men should be considered equal to one another. It was clear that this should include Black men and all women, but that in practice did not. But demanding the realization of the guiding principle of the country's formation did not require structural changes (i.e., revolution). It rather required the implementation of the principles that could be said to exist in the Declaration of Independence. In Iran, however, demands for freedom, democracy and respect for human rights are made within the framework of a constitution where an unelected supreme leader has absolute power over all layers of state, government and society. The system is structurally incapable of implementing the popular demands, and thus has to be removed. This is why the nature of the Green movement is revolutionary, and why its leaders, [Mir-Hossein] Musavi and [Mehdi] Karubi, have become liabilities.

Since the 1981 coup the [Iranian] regime lost its legitimacy with the majority of the public [and] . . . since then, Iran has been run by a counter-revolutionary regime.

The protests began to oppose a fraudulent election; the first slogan was "Where is my vote?" Why, within a few days, did the demonstrators turn from chanting slogans like 'death to dictator', 'independence, freedom, Iranian republic', to demanding regime change?

This is an interesting question. Why would a protest against a regime that supposedly came to power as a result of one of the most popular revolutions of the twentieth century so quickly turn to demand its removal? To answer that, we have to look at the history of the revolution, particularly the first two-and-a-half years. During this time, a fierce internal battle was waged between those who demanded that [Islamic Revolution leader Ayatollah Ruhollah] Khomeini fulfill his promises, made while in exile, to support the establishment of a democratic regime, on the one hand, and those seeking to establish a religious dictatorship. This struggle ended in a coup against the elected president, A.H. Banisadr, in June 1981. If we define the 1979 revolution according to its declared goals (the establishment of democracy and an Islamic discourse of freedom), then since the 1981 coup the regime lost its legitimacy with the majority of the public. We easily can argue that since then, Iran has been run by a counter-revolutionary regime.

This is well known to the regime, which is why after [former president Mohammad] Khatami's election and subsequent isolation within the regime, he not only failed to mobilize a mass movement to compensate his isolation within the regime, but even condemned the students uprising in 1998, which was spontaneously mobilized in his support. So the spontaneous protests against last year's vote rigging, in effect, just mirrored the actual nature of the public.

What do you think about rule of Iranians in Diaspora [Iranians living outside of Iran]? How significant are our actions in supporting the democratic movement in Iran?

I have yet to come across a social movement, in which the Diaspora did not play a key role. Before and during the Constitutional Revolution, the Iranian Diaspora in the Caucasus, Iraq and Europe played a major role. This was also the case during the nationalization of oil and more effectively in the 1979 revolution, when students outside Iran participated in the struggle. The role of Diaspora in this uprising is even more important than in the previous ones, not only because there has been a major increase in the numbers of Iranians living outside Iran, but also because the communication revolution has made it possible to communicate with Iranians inside Iran and exchange vital information. The regime's ability to shed blood has decreased because it can hardly hide its atrocities. We have very few photographs of Black Friday, for example, but many film clips of individuals killed by this regime. The coordination to expose the regime's brutality, between Iranians inside and outside Iran, is phenomenal.

The other role that the Diaspora has played is just as important as the first, if not more so. Many exiled intellectuals have widened the intellectual field of discussion about events happening within Iran, as they say things that those living within Iran cannot. Global public opinion is also vital for the movement, as it prevents governments from making secret deals with the Iranian regime. Exiled Iranians have thus been able to help mobilize global support for the movement through sharing uncensored information.

The Iranian Green Movement Is Not Revolutionary

Arshin Adib-Moghaddam

Arshin Adib-Moghaddam teaches comparative politics at the University of London and is the author of Iran in World Politics: The Question of the Islamic Republic.

D espite the systematic efforts of many commentators and media outlets to represent what is happening in Iran as a wholesale revolt against everything the Islamic Republic stands for, a sober analysis reveals that we are witnessing the renegotiation of political power in the country. The protagonists represent different wings within the system; the contours of their politics are drawn upon the expanding canvas of the Islamic Republic. In short: Iran is in a post-revolutionary state, not a pre-revolutionary one.

No Revolution for Iran

At the height of the demonstrations after the contested election of President Mahmoud Ahmadinezhad during last summer [2009], I argued, in an article that was disputed and challenged by many skeptics, that we were not witnessing another revolution. But simply because there is a consensus amongst many people with vested interests that the Islamic Republic must be subdued and vilified by any means, one should not be bullied into overlooking the nuances of the changing political landscape in Iran. Simply because the legitimate yearnings for democracy and justice by Iranians are misinterpreted as a rebellion against Iran's bias toward the Palestinian cause or indeed Islam itself, one should not be fooled into underestimating the capabilities of the state-sanctioned proponents of the political order in the country. What supporters of "regime change" can hope for, and what every Iranian, Arab, Muslim and any other person who empathizes with the plight of the people in the region must fear, is an entrenched civil war that would rip the country apart.

But I don't think it will come to that. We are already witnessing signs of accommodation. [Green movement leader] Mir-Hossein Mousavi has written a conciliatory letter, which was followed up by [conservative presidential candidate] Mohsen Rezai in his own communication with the Supreme Jurisprudent Ayatollah Ali Khamenei. Behind the curtains the political factions are negotiating in order to rescue the political system in Iran from further destabilization. The opposition figures, Mousavi, Mehdi Karroubi, Mohammad Khatami and most notably Ayatollah Ali Akbar Rafsanjani, emerged out of the revolution and would never devour the project they have been busy building up. They are disciples of the Islamic Republic, and they are revealing themselves as such at this very moment.

We were not witnessing another revolution [in Iran].

A Self-Confident Iranian Regime

There is a second reason why it is likely that the Iranian state and its vast underbelly will navigate through this crisis. The state has its destiny in its own hands, it was not placed where it is as the Shah was after the MI6/CIA [British and US intelligence agencies]–engineered coup d'etat in 1953 that deposed the democratically elected Prime Minister Mohammad Mossadegh and reinstalled the oppressive monarchy of [Shah] Mohammad Reza Pahlavi. So the Islamic Republic displays a totally different self-understanding. It perceives itself entirely capable and legitimized to assert its power and to dig in and defend itself by all means if necessary. It remains, despite the massive protests, rather self-confident.

A similar "indigenous" self-confidence animates the protesters. The movement in Iran is writing its own script. It is
steeped in the symbols of Iran's political culture and the very
language, adjusted to a different political reality, that perme-
ated the constitutional revolt in the country in 1906/1907, the
movement of the aforementioned Mohammad Mossadegh
and the Islamicized revolution itself. What we are witnessing
today, in other words, is a part of a long struggle in Iran for
government accountability and a system that is based on
popular legitimacy rather than transcendental entitlement.

---

*The "Green Movement" demands . . . the logical conclu-
sion of the [Islamic] revolutionary process . . . freedom
(azadi) from government oppression.*

A Struggle for Freedom

The Islamic Republic itself came into existence through a
popular mass movement, a plebiscite and a rhetoric that was
amenable to the demands of the populace. It reintroduced
electoral competition, however confined, supervised elections,
and instituted checks and balances within the system. It created a set of strategic preferences that were independent of
external dictates. And yet thus far it has failed to place itself
beyond the residues of authoritarianism in Iran. It has also
contributed to the demographics of the current protests: the
brave youngsters demonstrating on the streets and campuses
of Iran are a part of the "baby boom generation" born during
the Iran-Iraq war that benefitted from the vast expansion of
the higher education sector in the 1990s. The Islamic Republic, in other words, has created the very political reality it is
currently challenged by.

Iranians have managed to fulfill two of the promises of
the Islamic revolution: independence (esteghlal) and Islamic
Republic (jomhur-ye eslami). The "Green Movement" de-

mands nothing but the logical conclusion of the revolutionary process. What they demand is its third central promise: the great Utopia of freedom (azadi) from government oppression. This is by far the most difficult to attain, but the most valuable for a nation to strive for. Hence the ongoing protests and hence the willingness of Iranians to die for their just cause. This momentum will keep Iranian society going and it will decide whether or not Islam and democracy are finally reconcilable, in Iran and beyond.

The Iranian Green Movement Is a Civil Rights Movement

Hooman Majd

Hooman Majd, a New York-based writer, is author of the book
The Ayatollah Begs to Differ *(2008). He has also advised and
interpreted for two Iranian presidents, Mohammad Khatami
and Mahmoud Ahmadinejad, on their trips to the United States.*

The green movement is winning.

Yes, but over time. The answer depends on what "winning" means. One thing Western observers should have learned
from 30 years of second-guessing Iran and Iranians is that
second-guessing Iran and Iranians is often a mistake, and pre-
dicting the imminent demise of the Islamic theocracy is unrealistic.

What is evident is that if we consider Iran's pro-democracy
"green movement" not as a revolution but as a civil rights
movement—as the leaders of the movement do—then a "win"
must be measured over time. The movement's aim is not for a
sudden and complete overthrow of Iran's political system.
That may disappoint both extremes of the American and Iranian political spectrums, left and right, and especially U.S.
neoconservatives hoping for regime change.

Seen in this light, it's evident that the green movement has
already "won" in many respects, if a win means that many Iranians are no longer resigned to the undemocratic aspects of a
political system that has in the last three decades regressed,
rather than progressed, in affording its citizens the rights
promised to them under Iran's own Constitution.

The Islamic Republic's fractured leadership recognizes this, as is evident in its schizophrenic reaction to events since the disputed June [2009] election. Although the hard-liners in power may be able to suppress general unrest by sheer force, the leadership is also aware that elections in the Islamic state can never be held as they were in 2009 (even conservatives have called for a more transparent electoral system), nor can the authorities completely silence opposition politicians and their supporters or ignore their demands over the long term.

It augurs well for eventual democratic reform in Iran that the green movement continues to exist at all. Despite all efforts by the authorities to portray it as a dangerous counter-revolution, the green movement continues to attract supporters and sympathizers from even the clergy and conservative Iranians.

Many Iranians are no longer resigned to the undemocratic aspects of a political system that has in the last three decades regressed, rather than progressed.

The Green Movement Is Radicalizing

Only in part. It's important to remember that Iran's green movement began well before protests broke out in June 2009. The origins were in the *mowj-e-sabz*, also known as the "green wave," a campaign to support the presidential bid of reformist candidate Mir Hossein Mousavi, who ran against conservative incumbent Mahmoud Ahmadinejad.

The green wave's goals were to wrest the presidency and executive power away from radical hard-liners whose term in office had been marked by economic incompetence, foreign-policy adventurism, and an ideological doctrine that included new limits on civil rights and that Mousavi's supporters believed was unsuited to Iranian interests in the 21st century.

After the disputed election results, the green movement morphed from a political campaign into a campaign to annul the presidential election—and then, more broadly, into a movement to restore the civil liberties promised by the 1979 Islamic Revolution. With every instance of recent government tyranny, from show trials of opposition politicians and journalists to the beatings and murders of some demonstrators on Iran's streets, the movement has grown more steadfast in its demands for the rights of the people.

The radical elements claiming to be a part of the green movement only speak for a small minority of Iranians. The majority still want peaceful reform.

Over time, and particularly with the government's continued use of brutal force against its citizens, some Iranians are no longer satisfied with the stated goals of the green movement, but are looking to topple the Islamic regime altogether. For instance, we hear in the Western media many instances of Iranians clamoring for an "Iranian," rather than Islamic, republic (a call that Mousavi has disavowed) or for "death to the supreme leader." Meanwhile we see on YouTube and our TVs footage of Iranians violently confronting security forces.

However, the radical elements claiming to be a part of the green movement only speak for a small minority of Iranians. The majority still want peaceful reform of the system and not necessarily a wholesale revolution, bloody or otherwise. That's why, in the most recent Ashura demonstrations, for example, large groups of peaceful marchers actually prevented some of the movement's radicalized elements from beating or attacking security forces. Although accurate polling information is not available, based on what we hear and see of the leaders of the green movement and many of its supporters, radicalization is still limited to a minority of protesters.

The green movement's leaders recognize that any radicalization on their part will only bring down the state's iron fist. They are also cautious because they know that if movement leaders call for regime change rather than reform and adherence to the Constitution, they will only have proven the government's assertion that the movement's goal all along has been to topple the system.

The Revolutionary Guards Will Do Anything to Keep Khamenei in Power

Don't bet on it. The Revolutionary Guards [a branch of the Iranian military] are tasked with protecting the legacy of the 1979 Islamic Revolution and its embodiment in the *vali-e-faqih*, the supreme leader, currently Ayatollah Ali Khamenei.

The Guard's top leaders are military men who have served many years in the ranks and as such are unlikely to disobey the orders of their commander in chief. Their view, as they have expressed repeatedly in public fora, is that the green movement and its leaders are a threat to the revolution and to the supreme leader. But they are probably more concerned with protecting the *position* of the leader (and their own power and pervasive influence in Iranian business and politics) than they are in protecting a particular individual.

There are many former top commanders of the Guards, such as Mohsen Rezai (a defeated candidate in the presidential election), Mohammad Qalibaf (Tehran's popular mayor), and Ali Larijani (speaker of the parliament), who oppose Ahmadinejad (and have influence with the Guards), but have not so far challenged the supreme leader. That doesn't mean, though, that they would not look to replace Khamenei should it become apparent that he is an obstacle to the regime's stability. Although any moves against the supreme leader are highly unlikely at this point (and he still has the support of the majority of the members of the Assembly of Experts, the body that elects, monitors, and can even impeach him), that doesn't mean that such a challenge could never happen.

The Time for Compromise Is Over

Not in Iran, it ain't. The supreme leader, the Revolutionary Guards, and almost all of the hard-liners in government have said that they will tolerate no more dissent; they have said that there will be no compromise and that the green movement's demands will not be met. But that doesn't actually mean that some form of compromise isn't possible.

For starters, the green movement's leaders may recognize that they could become irrelevant if they are unwilling to either become more revolutionary (as some of their supporters already have), or compromise to protect the longevity of their movement as a civil rights campaign.

On Jan. 1 [2010], Mousavi listed the green movement's demands on civil rights and other reforms, but significantly he was no longer calling for an annulment of the 2009 election. Meanwhile, at the most recent meeting of the Expediency Council, the body that arbitrates disputes between Iran's executive and legislative branches, Mohsen Rezai, the conservative challenger to Ahmadinejad in the 2009 election, suggested that the government should listen to Mousavi's demands, describing them as "constructive." (Some Iran observers say the green movement is leaderless and argue that a headless movement will ultimately fail. And yet we're still hearing chants of "Ya Hossein, Mir Hossein!" at every protest. That's Mousavi.)

Both sides realize that the continuing unrest threatens the country's stability and that neither side is looking to reform the regime into oblivion. The current standoff makes no one happy. The odds aren't horrible that some form of compromise might occur in 2010, a compromise that would allow both sides to claim advances if not outright victory.

The Green Movement Wants or
Needs Foreign Support

Dead wrong. Nothing could be further from the truth. It is insulting and patronizing to suggest, as many commentators do, that without foreign help or support the green movement cannot be successful, that Iranians on their own are incapable of commanding their own destiny.

U.S. President Barack Obama has so far expressed only moral support for Iranians fighting for their civil rights and has rightly articulated the unrest in Iran as a purely Iranian affair. Lacking relations with Iran, Obama can do little to help the green movement, but plenty to hurt it. Coming out squarely on the side of the opposition in Iran is likely to undermine its credibility, and perhaps even lend credence to the government's assertion that the movement is a foreign-inspired plot that will rob Iran of its independence.

That the green movement has survived, and even grown, in the absence of foreign support (even moral support in its inception) is evidence that Iranians are perfectly capable of maintaining a civil rights movement and agitating for democratic change without the prodding, influence, or support of foreigners. Furthermore, if there is only one aspect of the Islamic Revolution that almost all Iranians can agree on as positive, it's that key events, such as the spontaneous unrest after the election and all the way back to the revolution itself, have happened independent of foreign influence.

The green movement is most definitely real, cannot be completely suppressed, and will undoubtedly have a long-term effect on the politics of the Islamic Republic.

The most potentially damaging accusation the government has made against the green movement is that it is a foreign plot to foment a "velvet" or "color" revolution that will once again render Iran subservient to a greater power. But this accusation has not stuck because the movement's leaders have always eschewed any foreign support and framed their fight as a purely Iranian one.

The idea that foreign support is either necessary or important to the green movement's ability to achieve its goals is as preposterous as imagining, say in 1965, that overt Soviet support of the civil rights movement in the United States was necessary for that movement to be successful.

For observers sitting in the United States or anywhere outside Iran, it is tempting to draw conclusions about the green movement or even the health of the Islamic regime based on what little information we are able to gather and what various analysts believe, given the extreme restrictions Iran has placed on journalists and reporting from Iran. However, Iran often defies expectations and has proven maddeningly immune from adhering to conventional wisdom. Listen to an Iranian exile opposed to the Islamic regime for five minutes and you'll be convinced that the regime's days are numbered not in years, but in months. Listen to a regime apologist for five minutes and you might be persuaded that Western powers are indeed fomenting the revolt and that the government will weather the storm and emerge as powerful as ever.

The truth, of course, always lies somewhere in between. The green movement is most definitely real, cannot be completely suppressed, and will undoubtedly have a long-term effect on the politics of the Islamic Republic. What began with the election of reformist President Mohammad Khatami in 1997 has finally culminated in a civil rights movement that by any name will continue to put pressure on the regime to reform, pressure that it can only ignore at the peril of its own demise.

The Iranian Green Movement Is a Twitter Revolution

Jared Keller

Jared Keller is an associate editor for The Atlantic *and* The Atlantic Wire *website and has written for various other publications.*

At the height of mass post-election protests that took place a year ago [2009] this month [June 2010] in Iran, known as the "Green Revolution," Western media outlets were filled with a flurry of reports of protesters using Twitter, e-mail, blogs, and text messages to coordinate rallies, share information, and locate compatriots. Journalists were agape at the sudden influx of information coming out of the country, unusual in light of the Iranian authorities' media blackout. "The immediacy of the reports was gripping," reported the *Washington Times*. "Well-developed Twitter lists showed a constant stream of situation updates and links to photos and videos, all of which painted a portrait of the developing turmoil. Digital photos and videos proliferated and were picked up and reported in countless external sources safe from the regime's Net crackdown." Journalists even gave the unrest in Tehran [Iran's capital] a second moniker: the "Twitter Revolution."

The Role of Twitter

But was there really a "Twitter Revolution?" *Radio Free Europe*'s Golnaz Esfandiari recently described the idea in *Foreign Policy* as "an irresistible meme [vehicle for cultural ideas] during the post-election protests, a story that wrote itself." Esfandiari explained that opposition activists primarily utilized text messages, email, and blog posts to organize protests, while "good old-fashioned word of mouth" was the most influential medium for coordinating opposition. Social media tools like Facebook and Twitter were not ideal for rapid communication among protesters, and utilized more by observers in other countries. "Western journalists who couldn't reach—or didn't bother reaching?—people on the ground in Iran simply scrolled through the English-language tweets posted with tag #iranelection," quipped Esfandiari. "Through it all, no one seemed to wonder why people trying to coordinate protests in Iran would be writing in any language other than Farsi."

While Twitter failed as an organizational tool, the Green movement remains the first major world event broadcast worldwide almost entirely via social media.

The concept of a "Twitter Revolution," as challenged by Esfandiari and others, is rooted in the idea that Twitter was the lifeblood of the Green Revolution. Taking this definition, Esfandiari and other critics are right: Twitter was no secret weapon that magically made the Islamic Republic disappear. "Twitter cannot stop a bullet," mused [political commentator] Charles Krauthammer on the Green Revolution's anniversary. "There was a lot of romantic outpouring here thinking that Facebook is going to stop the Revolutionary Guards [a branch of the Iranian military]. It doesn't. Thuggery, a determined regime that is oppressive, that will shoot, almost always wins." Social media tools like Facebook and Twitter, now our bread and butter, were more influential in mobilizing Diaspora [expatriate] Iranians and international observers in solidarity rather than coordinating street protests inside Iran.

A Twitter Revolution

But while Twitter failed as an organizational tool, the Green movement remains the first major world event broadcast worldwide almost entirely via social media. Given the extent of the Iranian regime of repression, the amount of information publicized real-time through social networks allowed the international community an unprecedented peek into the turmoil afflicting Iran. For the Greens, the international reaction to the post-election violence gave the movement critical international visibility. While crowd sourcing is now a familiar concept to even the marginally tech-savvy, Twitter's use on a massive scale was rarely contemplated nor executed prior to the Iranian election. The Green revolution *was* a Twitter revolution; while social media fell short organizationally, it brought the violence in the streets of Tehran to the forefront of the geopolitical conversation.

The unprecedented use of Twitter also situated the micro-blogging service at the center of a global social transformation. The Green Revolution was far from social media's political coming-out party; Barack Obama's media-centric 2008 presidential campaign was an early testing ground for new media as a means for political communication and organization, and the practices pioneered there quickly spread to other political movements around the globe. But it was the critical role of Twitter as a lightning rod for international attention that established it as a tool for political communication rather than outright organization. Iran's post-election unrest was the micro-blogging service's baptism by fire as a means to observe, report, and record, real-time, the unfolding of a crisis.

The Green revolution was *a Twitter revolution.*

Since the Iranian election protests, Twitter has provided eyes and ears in the direst situations. The earthquakes in Haiti and Chile earlier this year [2010] provided striking examples. With Haiti's communications infrastructure virtually obliterated and cell phones an inconsistent lifeline, Twitter and other social media provided a glimpse of conditions on the ground. [World news source] Mashable's Ben Parr reported that thousands of Facebook and Twitter updates appeared every minute, while Twitter was used to disseminate "moving and gut-wrenching TwitPics of the disaster." Following the 8.8 magnitude quake in Chile, Victor Herrero of *USA Today* wrote that in [the city of] Conception, the epicenter of the quake "social-networking tools such as Twitter, Facebook and some Google applications have been at the forefront of transmitting highly localized information . . . about finding families and friends, food and water, ways to get transportation." As in Iran, Haitians and Chileans used social media to create a mosaic of the human drama on the ground. And the medium's potential as an organizational tool continues to evolve, as we've seen in the case of South Korea's recent elections, narrowly overlapping with the anniversary of last year's political unrest in Iran.

The Green Revolution in Iran was muzzled, sadly, although the movement continues to put pressure on the Iranian regime a year after its initial protests. The Twitter Revolution, however, is far from over.

CHAPTER 2

Has Iran's Green Movement Been Destroyed?

Chapter Preface

Iran's military and security forces are the tools that the Iranian government authorities use to suppress antigovernment protests and challenges to the current Islamic regime. Iran has two primary branches of the military—the Islamic Republic of Iran Army (called Artesh, Farsi for army) and the Army of the Guardians of the Islamic Revolution (called the Revolutionary Guards)—both under the direct control of Iran's religious leaders. The Artesh is the regular Iranian army, which is charged mainly with defending Iran from external threats. It includes ground, air, naval, and cyber warfare capabilities and was the main fighting force during the war between Iran and Iraq in the 1980s. The Revolutionary Guards, on the other hand, is a separate army organized after the 1979 Islamic Revolution to protect the new government from internal unrest and uprisings. It reportedly has about 125,000 members, including ground, air, and naval forces, and it also controls a much larger auxiliary militia group known as the Basij. It is the feared Basij that most often enforces Islamic laws and metes out beatings, killings, and other punishments to suppress any type of challenge to the government.

The Basij was initially used by the Iranian regime in the 1980s to defend Iran during the Iran-Iraq War. Hundreds of thousands of Basij volunteers were sent to war zones to participate in human-wave attacks on Iraqi troops in the final years of the war. Human-wave attacks were a tactic in which large numbers of people attack enemy positions with few weapons—basically using people as cannon fodder, a tactic that caused massive numbers of casualties for Iran. At least partly because of the great sacrifices made by Basij members during the war, the group was made part of the Iranian military system at the war's end and reorganized into a domestic security force.

Today, the Basij is composed of volunteers who are considered to be extremely loyal to Iran's ruling religious leaders. Basij members are dispersed geographically and throughout Iranian society. There are armed wings as well as specialized units such as the Pupil Basij, the Student Basij, the University Basij, the Public Service Basij, and the Tribal Basij. Together, these Basij members—mostly young, poor, religious Iranians—work to uphold Islamic values and reinforce support for the Islamic regime. This work includes beneficial activities such as helping the elderly but also various forms of repression and intimidation. Basij members, for example, arrest women who violate the Islamic dress codes, enforce the religious rules against male-female fraternization, confiscate prohibited forms of entertainment materials, and harass government critics and intellectuals. Some observers have characterized the Basij as a type of secret police, because it is used as the eyes and ears of the regime to spy on citizens and keep them in line.

In recent years, armed Basij groups have also been used to physically attack, beat, and kill people who participate in street protests against the regime. The Basij has been credited with suppressing student uprisings in 1999, for example, and Basij members were also mobilized along with local police during the 2009 green movement protests. During these protests, Basij members armed with batons, knives, and rifles rushed into crowds of protesters and took aim from rooftops and other locations, attempting to disperse them with threats and acts of violence. In 2010, selected Basij members were also reportedly schooled in blogging and combating threats to the regime from the Internet. No one knows for sure how many Basij members there are in Iran, but some reports suggest that the Basij may consist of about 1.5 million men and women of military age. Although the levels of training vary significantly, some members of the Basij do receive training in riot-control tactics, which are used to respond to domestic uprisings. Some experts, however, have said that relatively un-trained Basij troops proved to be ineffective against the 2009 demonstrations; Basij members often responded brutally against protesters, generating public anger that could damage the regime in the long run, these experts assert.

Nevertheless, the Basij and other security forces were able to quell the 2009 and 2010 green movement uprisings against the Iranian regime. Whether the movement has been perma-nently destroyed or will live to fight another day is the subject of the viewpoints contained in this chapter.

The Iranian Green Movement Has Been Stifled Temporarily

Hossein Aryan

Hossein Aryan is deputy director of Radio Free Europe/Radio Liberty's Persian-language Radio Farda.

The events that have roiled Iran since the disputed June 12, 2009, presidential election are unprecedented in the 31-year history of the Islamic republic. Never before have citizens protested in such numbers to demand their rights be respected. In spite of repression, torture, widespread arrests, and even killings by the regime, the people took to the streets, although intermittently.

And never before have the rifts among the ruling factions been so noticeable.

Iran's Green Movement does not seem to be a passing phenomenon, and it has taken both hard-line regime elements and Western observers by surprise.

The turbulence in Iran should not be viewed as a clash between reformists with secularist tendencies and an entrenched ruling clique. It is, rather, a power struggle between two camps.

"Window Dressing"

In one camp is Supreme Leader Ayatollah Ali Khamenei, President Mahmud Ahmadinejad, [conservative cleric] Ayatollah Mesbah Yazdi, the Islamic Revolutionary Guards Corps (IRGC [a branch of the Iranian military]), and senior hard-line clerics who advocate for the status quo and a vigorous clampdown against the protests.

"Elected institutions are anathema to a religious government," Yazdi, who is Ahmadinejad's spiritual mentor, said last July [2009], "and should be no more than window dressing."

In early August, railing against protesters and opponents in a speech to the Association of Basij Scholars in Mashhad, Ahmadinejad said, "Let the swearing-in ceremony occur, and then we will take them by the collar and slam their heads into the ceiling."

For the time being, the [Iranian] regime has surmounted the crisis over its authority, but shadows still hang over its legitimacy.

The opposite camp, known as the Green Movement, comprises reformists and pragmatists who gravitate toward [Iranian politicians] Mir Hossein Musavi, Mehdi Karrubi, Ali Akbar Hashemi Rafsanjani, Mohammad Khatami, the Militant Clerics Association, and other moderate clerics. It must not be forgotten that the leaders of this camp fully support the Islamic regime and seek ways of reconciling the people and the state.

The fissures that emerged in the ranks of the political and clerical elite after the presidential election has widened and is now more visible than ever. Khamenei's backing of Ahmadinejad and his hasty endorsement of the election results provoked protests that dented the legitimacy of the regime and Khamenei's authority.

For the time being, the regime has surmounted the crisis over its authority, but shadows still hang over its legitimacy. Khamenei knows that it will take more than continued repression to maintain the security of the regime. At the same time, though, the Green Movement made a weaker-than-expected showing on February 11 [2010] when the 31st anniversary of the founding of the Islamic republic was expected to serve as a pretext for mass demonstrations. Since then, the regime has been working on new strategies to solidify its position.

Greens Are Fragmented

The Green Movement is not merely about Musavi and Karrubi. It is an amorphous amalgamation of various groups and people, espousing a wide range of political philosophies and goals.

The ability of the [Green] Movement to sustain itself and generate intermittent rallies, in spite of its fragmentation, is the most remarkable aspect of what we have seen in Iran.

Some, like Musavi, want to reclaim the revolution within the framework of the current constitution. Others want to strengthen the elements of republicanism and democracy within the exiting order. And there are also people within the Green Movement who see an opportunity to do away with the Islamic regime entirely.

As a result, the Green Movement is fragmented. It lacks the kind of structure that the opposition to the shah had in 1979. It is local, sporadic, and does not have a central nervous system or a coherent ideology. However, this should be little comfort to the regime, because the longer the movement survives and holds together, the more it is likely to produce its own leaders. In fact, the ability of the movement to sustain itself and generate intermittent rallies, in spite of its fragmentation, is the most remarkable aspect of what we have seen in Iran since last June.

However, the movement has not been able to garner broad support among bazaar merchants, labor unions, and other social groups. Musavi emphasized this shortcoming in his Norouz message, saying the Green Movement must expand its reach to all segments of society.

The protests in Iran seem to be stuck in a rut, although on December 27 (Ashura [Muslim holiday]) the demonstrations spread to a number of smaller cities for the first time. But the social composition of the demonstrators remains the same: They are largely young (many of them are women), well-dressed, and educated with mobile phones and Internet 2.0 skills (YouTube, Facebook, Twitter, etc.).

Four Layers of Security

Nonetheless, the regime is treating the Green Movement as a serious threat to its authority. It has four layers of security forces to maintain domestic security, protect the regime, and deal with any unrest. The first layer is the Law Enforcement Force (police force).

The second is the Basij Resistance Force (BRF), [a militia group] with a nominal strength of 13.6 million, of which about 1.5 million men and women with basic military and riot-control training can be easily deployed. The backbone of this force is 1905 Ashura, 446 Al-Zahra (for women), and 259 Iman Hussein battalions, as well as some 52,000 Karbala and Zolfaqar combat groups. The head of the Basij militia is directly subordinate to the commander of the IRGC.

The third layer—the most resolute group—is the IRGC, which now numbers 120,000. As well as being a major player in the political and military arenas, the IRGC is an economic juggernaut and the largest beneficiary of government contracts. Many former commanders of this force have taken senior positions in the executive branch, especially in the Intelligence and Interior ministries.

The enmity of these commanders toward the reformists or toward any effort to change the status quo became evident in July 1999 when student protests in Tehran [capital of Iran] convinced them (and Khamenei) that then-President [Mohammad] Khatami's reformist agenda was too great a threat to the Islamic regime. As a result, 24 IRGC commanders sent Khatami a letter criticizing his reform efforts and accusing him of endangering the revolutionary order.

In their letter, the signatories said they were reserving the right to interfere in politics in the name of their mandate to protect the Islamic regime. The letter was largely viewed as a direct threat of a coup, and one of the signatories was Major General Mohammad Ali Jafari, the current IRGC commander.

The fourth layer of regime security is the military (Artesh), with 430,000 troops. This force, assigned to protect the country's borders, plays no political role and is unlikely to suppress domestic unrest.

Crucial Security Arrangements

Most of the protests over the last 10 months have taken place in Tehran Province, and security arrangements there are crucial for the regime. And the Basij militia is playing the key role. Recently, in order to provide for better coordination with policy in the event of unrest, the IRGC divided the Tehran Basij into 22 units, one for each district of the capital (previously, there were six Basij units there). Greater Tehran has a population of about 8.5 million people, while the entire province is home to about 12 million.

Overall command responsibility for dealing with unrest in Tehran is vested in the Sarollah Headquarters, which controls two elite divisions of the IRGC and all the Basij militia and police units in the entire province. The IRGC's Mohammad Rasulallah Division is charged with maintaining security throughout greater Tehran, while the Seyyed ol-Shohada Division has responsibility for the rest of the province.

The Sarollah Headquarters is commanded by the head of the IRGC and acts under the direct orders of the supreme leader. It receives intelligence from the Intelligence Ministry, the intelligence branch of the police force, and the newly enlarged Intelligence Organization of the IRGC itself. The latter handles a number of tasks, including waging the cybercampaign against the Green Movement and foreign media that are viewed as waging a "soft-power war" against the Islamic republic.

Encouraged by the success of the Ashura protests in December [2010], the Greens were expected to stage even larger protests on the February anniversary of the founding of the Islamic republic. Musavi and Karrubi both called for people to take to the streets for protests to coincide with the anniversary.

However, the government was well prepared this time. Khamenei denounced the opposition as "counterrevolutionaries" who were being exploited by the country's foreign enemies—the United States, Great Britain, and Israel. Iranians "will punch them in their mouths to shock them," Khamenei said. In the end, the regime held its anniversary celebrations and prevented the opposition from staging significant protests.

The regime itself is ... not entirely immune to the arguments of the Green Movement or the public's bitterness at the failure of the regime to provide freedom and prosperity.

A Thorn in the Side

Though not an existential threat, the Green Movement has been a major thorn in the side of the regime. However, the poor performance of the movement in February indicates the regime is gaining the upper hand. Khamenei's Norouz message to the nation, in which he condemned the protesters and those who support them, indicated that he has regained much of his authority, although the regime's legitimacy remains in doubt.

The regime seems to be holding the Green Movement in check, which has activists frustrated. The Greens have no open means of organizing their supporters, developing a long-term strategy, or airing their views. They remain under siege. Building "the desired society requires patience, perseverance, and endurance against the hardships and challenges ahead," Musavi told a group of activists on April 22. "We must create a coherent civil society using all available resources in the country."

However, none of the outstanding issues of Iran's domestic situation that have been highlighted by the Green Movement has been resolved, meaning that the regime remains vulnerable. Among these issues, I'd list rivalries for power, disagreement on the balance between religious and republican elements of the regime, political differences among leading clerics, and disagreements on economic policies.

IRGC commanders will continue to act to keep Khamenei in power, but this does not mean that they will not consider replacing him if he is judged to be a liability or a threat to the preservation of the regime. But the regime itself is not a monolith, and the IRGC and the Basij are not entirely immune to the arguments of the Green Movement or the public's bitterness at the failure of the regime to provide freedom and prosperity.

It is always difficult to predict the future in Iranian politics, but I'd argue the most likely scenario for the next few years could be a continuation of the current war of attrition between the regime and the Green Movement or its successors. The regime will continue to deny the opposition the ability to challenge it effectively, while being unable to eliminate the sources of the discontent fuelling the Green protests. At the same time, it would be unrealistic to expect the demise of the regime any time soon, unless the Green Movement develops new methods of organizing itself, capitalizing on its gains, and broadening its appeal.

The Idea of an Iranian Revolution Was Always Unrealistic

Fareed Zakaria

Fareed Zakaria is a columnist at Newsweek *and is editor of* Newsweek International, *an international version of the magazine.*

As Barack Obama goes through one of his most difficult periods as president, you might wonder what it would have been like if the other guy had won. We will never know, of course, but in one area John McCain provides us with some clues. He would have tried to overthrow the government of Iran. In a June 10 speech, later published as a cover essay in the *New Republic*, McCain urged that we "unleash America's full moral power" to topple the Tehran regime. The speech highlights one of the crucial failings of McCain's worldview, one in which rhetoric replaces analysis and fantasy substitutes for foreign policy.

It has become something of a mantra among neoconservatives that we missed a chance to transform Iran a year ago. Reuel Marc Gerecht, writing in the *New York Times* last week, compares Iran's Green Movement to "what transpired behind the Iron Curtain in the 1980s" and accuses President Obama of being passive in the face of this historical moment. *Wall Street Journal* columnist Bret Stephens imagines that a more forceful Western response could have set off a revolution.

I have been deeply supportive of Iran's Green Movement. I wrote about it, highlighted it on television and showcased its advocates. But I do not think it was likely to overthrow the

Iranian regime. To believe that, one has to believe the government in Tehran is deeply unpopular with a majority of Iranians, holds onto power through military force alone and is thus vulnerable to a movement that could mobilize the vast majority in Iran who despise it. None of this is entirely true.

The Iranian regime has many, many opponents, but it also has millions of supporters. Mahmoud Ahmadinejad may have actually lost the presidential election of 2009, but it was a close contest in which he got millions of votes. What little polling has been done in Iran, coupled with the observations of people who have been there, all suggest that the regime has considerable public support in rural areas, among the devout and in poorer communities. *Newsweek's* Maziar Bahari, who was jailed by the government for four months on trumped-up charges, believes that Supreme Leader Ayatollah Ali Khamenei remains the most popular political figure in Iran.

McCain reveals a startling ignorance about the Iranian regime when he argues, as in his speech, that it "spends its people's precious resources not on roads, or schools, or hospitals, or jobs that benefit all Iranians—but on funding violent groups of foreign extremists who murder the innocent." While Tehran does fund militant groups, one of the keys to Ahmadinejad's popularity has been his large-scale spending on social programs for the poor. The regime lays out far more money on those domestic programs than on anything abroad.

The Iranian regime has many, many opponents, but it also has millions of supporters.

The comparison of Iran's Green Revolution to the velvet revolutions of Eastern Europe is mistaken. In 1989 dissidents had three forces on their side: nationalism (because communism had been imposed by force by a foreign power), religion (because communism repressed the church) and democracy. The Green Movement has only one: democracy. The regime

61

has always used the religiosity of the people to its advantage, but it has also become skilled at manipulating nationalism.

In May, Akbar Ganji was awarded, by a selection committee in which I take part, the Milton Friedman Prize for Advancing Liberty. Ganji, one of the bravest advocates of nonviolent agitation and secular democracy for Iran, was jailed for six years in Evin Prison, mostly in solitary confinement, for his writings against the government. In his acceptance speech, Ganji explained that U.S. foreign policy does have an impact on Iran's freedom movement but not quite in the sense that neoconservatives mean.

"Even entertaining the possibility of a military strike, especially when predicated on the nuclear issue," Ganji said, "is beneficial to the fundamentalists who rule Iran. As such, the idea itself is detrimental to the democratic movement in my country." The regime bends international issues to its favor and has become vocal about what Ganji calls the "gushing wound of Palestine . . . [which] worsens the infection of fundamentalism." He pointed out that Tehran continually reminds Iranians of America's "double standards" in opposing Iran's nuclear program while staying silent about Israel's arsenal of atomic weapons.

Ironically, those hoping to liberate Iranians are the same people urging punitive sanctions and even military force against Iran. Do they think that when the bombs hit, those who wear green will be spared?

Iran's Green Movement Is Not Dead

Michael Singh

Michael Singh is a fellow at the Washington Institute for Near East Policy in Washington, DC.

On June 10, when the Iranian opposition movement cancelled its planned commemoration of the anniversary of Mahmoud Ahmadinejad's disputed reelection, commentators assumed that the Green Movement was finally finished. For months, it had been criticized as lacking strong leadership and for being unable to seriously challenge Iran's entrenched regime.

But the history of political turmoil in twentieth-century Iran suggests that the movement may yet survive. After all, movements propelled by similar social currents have succeeded in dramatically changing Iran in the past.

Three periods of domestic political turbulence shook Iran in the last century—the Constitutional Revolution of 1905–11, which for a time curbed royal power and led to the development of Iran's constitution; the Muhammed Mossadeq era of 1951–3, which temporarily ousted Mohammad Reza Shah Pahlavi; and the 1979 Islamic Revolution, which replaced the monarchy with clerical rule.

Each of these episodes was brought about by the confluence of three factors: increasing popular anger at the regime's corruption, a rupture between the ruling and clerical classes, and dissatisfaction with Iran's foreign relations. In each instance, two disparate camps—one secular and liberal, the other comprised of politically active (often young and mid-ranking) clergy—momentarily came together in opposition.

Indeed, although periods of upheaval tend to be remembered today as being driven by iconic leaders such as Mossadeq, in the 1950s, and Ayatollah Ruhollah Khomeini, in 1979, it is important not to forget how broad and longstanding the popular movements behind them actually were.

The history of political turmoil in twentieth-century Iran suggests that the movement may yet survive.

In the early 1900s, for example, long-simmering outrage at the shah's tyrannical behavior and humiliating trade concessions to Russia and Great Britain boiled over when the director of customs (a Belgian national) began to enforce tariffs to pay off Russian loans. Intellectuals were joined by clerics, for whom the concessions were not only an affront to Islam but also a threat to the economic interests of religious endowments. The two camps came together to demand the ouster of the shah's prime minister and the establishment of a parliament. In the 1950s, nationalist revolutionaries campaigned to rid Iran of British control, citing the Anglo-Iranian Oil Company as a symbol of imperialist exploitation. Mossadeq spearheaded the movement but relied on Ayatollah Sayed Abol-Ghasem Kashani to rally an activist segment of the clergy. Kashani's example may have been an inspiration to Khomeini, who, in the 1960s and 1970s, brought together an extensive coalition, including secularists, clerics, youth, and others. In demanding an end to the monarchy, Khomeini and his associates seized on widespread disgust at the shah's coziness with Western powers and outrage over his oppressive and corrupt behavior. The coalition was galvanized by Mohammad Reza's land reforms, which threatened the financial base of clerics and other wealthy elites.

All three opposition movements took years to consolidate before becoming powerful enough to force change on the regime. The Constitutional Revolution, which is thought of as emerging around 1905, as protests broke out over tariffs, was in fact a continuation of events that began in 1891, with the campaign to overturn an exclusive tobacco concession the shah had granted to the British. Similarly, Mossadeq's National Front achieved power in 1951, but this was after decades of discontent with a monarchy that had descended into disorder following World War II. The violence of this era was a long-standing family feud as well: before ousting Mohammad Reza in 1951, Mossadeq had been imprisoned by Mohammad Reza's father—Reza Shah—for, among other things, casting a dissenting vote in the parliament in 1925 against his coronation. The Islamic Revolution of 1979, moreover, had roots going back to 1960–4, when riots against the shah swept the country and Ayatollah Khomeini and many other activists were exiled.

Just as reform movements past were slow to build, today's cannot be declared over because of the Green Movement's apparent sluggishness.

Each period of turmoil was distinctive but was propelled by similar undercurrents. It is a peculiar irony that in today's campaign against Khomeini's political heirs, the opposition movement is appealing to many of the same grievances Khomeini cited in his campaign against the shah. And indeed, the very same three factors that contributed to previous episodes of turbulence are converging again today. First, Ahmadinejad's apparent theft of the 2009 presidential election, and the regime's harsh repression of protests and other dissent preceding and following those elections, have fueled accusations of corruption and tyranny. This displeasure has been exacerbated by the popular perception that a privileged few—mainly elites in the Islamic Revolutionary Guard Corps—have benefited from Iran's resource wealth while average citizens have struggled. Second, the mounting international opprobrium directed at Tehran has created a sense that the regime's mismanagement of foreign relations is an embarrassment and harmful to Iran's interests. Finally, the clergy appear to be dissatisfied with the government (exemplified for now less by active opposition than by the dwindling clerical representation in government and the growing number of clergy who refrain from political activism on behalf of the regime), and some of the citizenry have even accused the regime of being "un-Islamic" for its policies of repression and torture.

This movement, too, is wide-ranging. It brings together not only reformists associated with Muhammad Khatami's more liberal government of the late 1990s but also former conservative stalwarts, such as Mir Hussein Moussavi, the movement's leader. It also appears to be at least tacitly aligned with other hardliners, such as former President Ali Akbar Hashemi Rafsanjani, and with quiescent clergy, labor activists, students, and merchants who have grown unhappy with the regime's economic policies. All seek to curtail corruption, restore a greater measure of civil rights to Iranians, and establish a less dangerous, more productive relationship with the outside world.

Moreover, the Green Movement is built on discontent that predates the June 2009 elections: it is the same dissatisfaction that led to Khatami's landslide electoral victories in 1997 and 2001 and to the student protests between the late 1990s and today. Just as reform movements past were slow to build, today's cannot be declared over because of the Green Movement's apparent sluggishness. The mass protests following Ahmedinejad's election have shown that regime has lost the affection of the majority of Iranians. So even as questions persist about the Green Movement's viability, the regime's viability is no clearer.

Yet if history gives cause for optimism regarding the opposition's prospects for success, it also gives cause for caution. Their primary goals achieved, the coalitions leading the past century's three reform movements quickly crumbled, riven by conflicting objectives and ideologies. After the Constitutionalists ousted the shah's prime minister and convened a parliament, they quickly found themselves pitted against clergy advocating an Islamic state. By 1911, Russian troops had shelled and disbanded the parliament, leading clerics had been executed, and Iran was controlled by the Russians in the north and the British in the south. Two years after coming to power, the coalition led by the National Front was similarly fractured, and communist partisans were the strongest force in the streets. A U.S.- and British-organized coup soon ousted Mossadeq. And finally, in the months after the Islamic republic was established, Khomeini's Iran plunged into bloody violence between competing factions. The regime likely only survived due to the unifying effect of the war with Iraq in 1980.

The international community should not worry that the Green Movement is doomed, but it should harbor no illusions that its success would inevitably lead to peace and democracy in the long term. Indeed, the United States and its allies should be considering not only how best to support the democratic aspirations of Iranians but also how to prepare for the real possibility of instability in Iran should the opposition prevail.

The Iranian Green Movement Is Alive

James Miller

James Miller is the creator of Dissected News, a news and politics website.

On June 12, 2009, Iran's now infamous elections were held where hardline President Mahmoud Ahmadinejad allegedly won with 62% of the vote. What resulted was a momentous period of time where Iranian dissidents voiced their opposition to the results and to the government itself, against all odds and at great personal risk.

On June 7th, 2010, *Foreign Policy* Magazine published an eight-part series called "Misreading Tehran: Leading Iranian-American writers revisit a year of dreams and discouragement." It was written by mainstream journalists criticizing what were common assertions during the post-election events: that Twitter was leading a "Revolution," that the regime was about to collapse, that the Green Movement would change everything by using technology to democratize democracy, and that Westerners could sit in their offices and homes and make a difference, 140 characters at a time. None of these things, according to some critics, were true. And so the conclusion must be that the Green Movement disappeared or has become insignificant since last summer. Technology (Twitter, social networking, new media, etc.), therefore, cannot really democratize a revolution. According to the media, all of the promise of post-election Iran has been lost.

But the critics saying these things, mainstream journalists, are really commenting on how mainstream journalism, for a brief moment, attempted to copy, catch up with, and comment on new media sources such as Twitter, Facebook, You-tube, and many blogs that were accomplishing what the old media could not. And in this rush to catch up, the media got it wrong. While many of these writers have very critical things to say about the new media's role in these events, they are already criticizing their previous belief systems surrounding the new media and the Green Movement.

The idea that the Green Movement would be successful in a few short months is ridiculous.

They neither understood then, nor understand now, the true significance of the so-called and misnamed "Twitter Revolution," or the grander significance of the Green Movement, or the real story in Iran.

The Green Movement Did Not Fail

Revolutions are not won in a day. The American Revolution was the product of over 100 years of philosophical thought, and several decades of discontent (the Stamp Act was passed in 1764, and by 1765 Patrick Henry was already a famous speaker), followed by several years of open rebellion and acts of defiance (Boston massacre in 1770, Boston Tea Party in 1773), and at least a year of open warfare (from Lexington Green to Breed's/Bunker Hill), all before the signing of the Declaration of Independence, the opening chapter to a formal war that lasted more than ten years. The "in-between" times were marked by backroom leadership, dinner table debate, church pulpit protests . . . democracy in an incubator. The idea that the Green Movement would be successful in a few short months is ridiculous, the product of the unbelievable promise and inspiring courage of the Iranian protesters crashing headlong into the ability for technology to spread the echoes of their "shot heard round the world" in an instant. Looking back, these hopes were naive, and the condemnation of their disappointment profoundly arrogant.

Dr. Scott Lucas, a former adjunct professor at an Iranian university and Professor of American Studies at the University of Birmingham (England), sums it up succinctly:

> Prize fights are settled within 15 rounds of three minutes each; the quest for civil rights is not. The election, after all, was just the public apex of a larger, ongoing climb for political, economic, and social recognition, respect, and justice. The Green Movement, as significant as it would become, did not displace the movements for women's rights, student rights, labour rights, legal rights, economic rights, religious rights, and the rights of Iran's many ethnic groups. (Indeed, one of the ongoing, "deeper" issues of this past year has been how the Green Movement—if it is more than a symbolic entity—interacts with the activism of these other movements.)

> This post-election contest, which rested upon years of discussion and challenge within the Islamic Republic, was always destined to be a marathon and not a sprint.

A fledgling democratic movement has moved from the shadows, where it has been hunted for decades, and into the limelight.

Twitter wasn't the story last June, and it certainly isn't today. Twitter was always a tool for getting news out more than it was for getting news in (though its ability to get news to supporters on the streets has also been dismissed too easily). But the REAL story is that for the last year, a fledgling democratic movement has moved from the shadows, where it has been hunted for decades, and into the limelight. And then back out of it, which also doesn't matter. The movement has matured and grown, even though (like anything in an incubator) it has often struggled and foundered.

And what are the results of the struggle of the opposition movement in Iran? Not failure. Externally, the movement has inspired [US secretary of state] Hillary Clinton, America's foreign policy has evolved from the false dichotomy of "invade or ignore ([the policy of President George W.] Bush)" to one of fostering developing democratic movements through the use of technology and a "Three Cups of Tea" [a reference to a book that documents one man's efforts to build schools in Pakistan and Afghanistan] outreach process to people in Iran, Sudan, Cuba, Venezuela, China, and beyond. This process will take while, but internally, as a direct result of the Green Movement, the regime is getting weaker. There are now serious divides inside the Iranian regime. As unemployment mounts, inflation rises, the problems mentioned above go unresolved, and as the internet outreach of those who still care about the Green Movement continues, the future of Iran may be a successful revolution.

Gaining Ground

The most painful part of the media's quick dismissal of the opposition to the [President Mahmoud] Ahmadinejad/ [Supreme Leader Sayyid Ali] Khamenei regime is this: Those of us who follow Iran, who have contacts within Iran, and who spend hours a day following the news there, know that the movement is actually gaining ground. We see signs that the regime is showing cracks in its armor. But we also see the bravery and sacrifice of the Iranians dissidents, men and women whose names never make it to the media.

Men like Farzad Kamangar, "a 34-year-old teacher and social worker, who was charged with Moharebeh (taking up arms against God), convicted and sentenced to death in February 2008, after a seven-minute long trial in which 'zero evidence' was presented," [as reported by the International Campaign for Human Rights in Iran]. Then, there are men like journalist and human rights defender Emadeddin Baghi, who has been arrested and is lavishing in poor health in Evin prison for daring to report the brutal crackdown of a ruthless dictator.

That doesn't include the (at least) 48 protesters who died in the streets, and the four more who were tortured and killed in prison, for speaking their voice of discontent. It doesn't include the 388 who were executed last year, or the 34 protesters who have been sentenced to death for speaking against their government, or the 17 Kurds charged with "moharebeh" and tortured to confess, just because they are vocal leaders of a hated minority.

Or [innocent bystander and now Green Movement martyr] Neda [Agha-Soltan].

Those of us who follow Iran, who have contacts within Iran, and who spend hours a day following the news there, know that the [green] movement is actually gaining ground.

But the blood on the street means something. It means that the regime is sometimes forced into backing down. It means that some clerics are no longer afraid to question the authority of their government.

This is the real tragedy of the media coverage of Iran. Not only did they misrepresent the boat, and then miss the boat, but they missed the significance and importance of the boat. What we are talking about in Iran is a movement that could bring peace between Israel and Iran, unsanctioned trade between Iran and the rest of the world, and the replacement of one of our greatest enemies with a potentially great friend, without a single bullet being fired by the United States. Not only that, but the success of the Green Movement would be the first step in the victory against human rights abuses everywhere, abuses which stifle the democratic process and thus deny the rest of the world the next generation of peaceful neighbors.

By demonizing Iran for its nuclear program, the media has created a bugbear that has encouraged the warmongers and distorted the truth in the Middle East. These same pressures have forced [President Barack] Obama to risk destroying with his feet what he has built with his hands. The coverage of the Green Movement in Iran was a chance to break that narrative, and by having to retract a reckless, sexy story about social media, the news agencies have now reverted to their radioactive news cycle by dismissing the best hope for change in the region, and beyond.

The strength of the Green Movement in Iran is countless, and growing.

Human rights violations have hampered democracy in Iran, and with it the best chance for hope and change in the Middle East. The media wants to dismiss this, because long and complicated stories don't sell. War sells. Nukes sell. But I'm not buying.

The success of the democratic movement in Iran cannot be measured in Tweets, in newspaper stories, in rallies attended (or not attended) by reformists, or even in protesters. It must be counted in the desire for freedom and peace. As such, the strength of the Green Movement in Iran is countless, and growing.

Iranian Green Movement Supporters Will Not Quit

Omid Memarian and Roja Heydarpour

Omid Memarian was a World Peace Fellow at the University of California–Berkeley Graduate School of Journalism and is a columnist whose writing has appeared in the New York Times, Los Angeles Times, San Francisco Chronicle, *and other publications. Roja Heydarpour is an editor at The Daily Beast, an online news website.*

A man in Tehran [Iran's capital] climbed a crane about five stories tall Monday [February 14, 2011], waved pictures and symbols of Iran's green movement, and threatened to jump to his death. But police managed to arrest him before he became a martyr, like the man who set himself ablaze earlier this year, sparking Tunisia's revolution.

The Iranian was one of tens of thousands who poured into the streets of Tehran and other cities across the country, reinvigorated by the revolutions in Egypt and Tunisia. But unlike Egypt and Tunisia, Monday was Round 3 for Iran's protesters, whom authorities thought they had silenced through intense intimidation campaigns since the first outpouring in June 2009, after the allegedly fraudulent election of President Mahmoud Ahmadinejad.

In January alone, more than 70 Iranians were hanged on various charges. In the last two weeks, dozens of opposition leaders have either been arrested or become targets of monitoring, according to Human Rights Watch. Opposition leaders Mir-Hossein Mousavi and Mehdi Karroubi were placed under house arrest. This month, they requested a permit for protests but were denied.

Another Brutal Crackdown

But the protesters still came out Monday, along with the militias and riot police, despite low expectations due to severe crackdowns and police brutality. And while demonstrators wised up and tried new tactics, including a Facebook page that gained more than 60,000 fans in just over a week, like the one that helped start protests in Egypt, riot police changed their ways too, this time disguising themselves as young protesters.

Tens of thousands [of Iranians] . . . poured into the streets of Tehran and other cities across the country, reinvigorated by the revolutions in Egypt and Tunisia.

"The Basijis [secret police] were unrecognizable," a journalist told *The Daily Beast* on the condition of anonymity. "They went among the people and all of a sudden they would take someone by the hand and pull him on the ground. Unlike the last times, when they sported beards, they had styled hair and wore stylish clothes. I myself was hit with batons several times. After several hours, it still hurts where they hit me."

Electric batons, wooden bats, tear gas, and paintball bullets were all weapons of choice. The moment people stopped marching and formed a group, riot police came out, according to eyewitness accounts. And the moment they started chanting, there seemed to be more police than demonstrators.

Problems of Isolation

At first, information was particularly hard to get during these protests, the largest since December 2009. People from inside and outside the country frantically sent messages and tidbits of news through Twitter and Facebook, but at times it was difficult to discern what was true and what wasn't, not to mention the blocked sites and slow Internet connections. At one point, there was a flurry of messages, including one from Mousavi, asking people not to spread unconfirmed information.

Slogans emerged as the best timestamp for videos leaking onto the Internet. Among the more popular Monday: "Na Ghaza, na Lobnan; Tunis o Misr o Iran!" ("Not Gaza, not Lebanon; Tunisia and Egypt and Iran!") There was also: "Mubarak, Ben Ali, Nobateh Seyyed Ali" ("[Egypt's Hosni] Mubarak, [Tunisia's Zine el-Abidine] Ben Ali, now it's [Iran's Seyyed Ali] Khamenei's turn"). And as always, there were strong chants of "Death to the dictator!"

Iran's semi-official news agency Fars confirmed at least one death Monday and called demonstrators "hypocrites, monarchists, ruffians, and seditionists," blaming the West as well as the MEK, a reviled exiled group based in both Iraq and France.

And from Washington [DC], [US Secretary of State] Hillary Clinton condemned the violence. "We wish the opposition and the brave people in the streets across cities in Iran the same opportunity that they saw their Egyptian counterparts seize in the last week," she said.

Although the United States' condemnation is important, the sour relations between the two countries make the protesters' struggles more difficult, said Karim Sadjadpour of the Carnegie Endowment, a Washington-based think tank.

"American-backed autocracies, like Mubarak's Egypt, are more vulnerable than anti-American dictatorships like Iran, for they are subject to the scrutiny of American politics and public opinion," said Sadjadpour. "Iran can slaughter its people without worrying that China or Russia is going to hold it accountable or withhold aid money."

And there are no live streams over the square, as there was in Egypt, making sure the world is watching.

"Unlike Egypt, the international media is not able to report on such protests, so once people go to the streets, they turn off the lights and start beating and harassing people," one protester told *The Daily Beast*.

From prison, away from the lights, Issa Saharkhiz, a prominent journalist who was arrested shortly after the post-election demonstrations, wrote a letter to protesters across the region. "I would like to congratulate the freedom of the people of Tunisia and Egypt from the grip of their dictators," he wrote. "I hope that Iran's dictator is also made to leave, through the people's will.... I wish I could be among you and with you on this historical day."

It now appears that the Iranian regime's thinking about the end of street protests and the green movement's death were overly optimistic.

Aside from the imprisonment of its leaders and the isolation from the world, the green movement suffers from a lack of direction, said Sadjadpour. The Egyptians had a very clear demand: They wanted Mubarak out. In Iran, there is still some confusion about whether there should be another revolution—something many can't stomach just three decades after the last one, which overthrew the shah—or reform within the existing Islamic Republic.

"I don't think a critical mass of people is going to take to the streets and risk their lives for ambiguous ends," said Sadjadpour.

The Green Movement Is Still Alive

Still, Monday's showing came as a bit of surprise. The fear that the regime has injected into society seemed to be enough to nearly silence the opposition for over a year. But as people poured into the streets of Bahrain and Yemen, also inspired by Tunisia and Egypt, the Iranian youth seemed to have been invigorated as well.

"The post-election crackdown on Iranians was so large-scale, the regime repeatedly emphasized with self-confidence that the streets of Tehran and other cities would never see another public protest," said an analyst who worked with former President Mohammad Khatami's office, speaking on the condition of anonymity. "But today, following a call by the reformist leaders, tens of thousands of people from different areas embarked upon street protests in multiple locations. It now appears that the Iranian regime's thinking about the end of street protests and the green movement's death were overly optimistic."

CHAPTER 3

Is Iran's Green Movement Related to Uprisings in Tunisia and Egypt?

Chapter Preface

A number of developing nations have overthrown autocratic regimes and held democratic elections in recent decades, and one of the most recent examples of such a movement for democratic freedoms is Tunisia—a relatively small country in northern Africa bordered by Algeria to the west, Libya to the southeast, and the Mediterranean Sea to the north and east. Once under French colonial rule, Tunisia achieved independence in 1957, adopting a multiparty democratic system of government. Although technically a democracy, Tunisia has become known as one of the world's most autocratic states—a country where one party rules, human rights and freedom of the press are restricted, the Internet is censored, and political corruption is widespread. Tunisians have lived with such repression for decades, but this changed with the eruption of spontaneous protests against the government in December 2010. Tunisia's government was overthrown in January 2011, bringing hope for true democracy to the nation.

Tunisia has been controlled since the time of its independence by one political party—the Constitutional Democratic Rally (RCD). Since 1987, the country's president has been Zine el Abidine Ben Ali, a member of the RCD who has gained the reputation as one of the region's most repressive Arab leaders. Under his rule, Tunisia has been politically stable, and wealthy elites have lived well, but only at the expense of the country's poorer citizens, who have suffered from poor living conditions, high unemployment, and a lack of human rights and freedoms. Despite the president's autocratic rule, Tunisia's regime has been supported by the United States, largely because it has prevented the rise of radical Islam among its Arab population and helped western nations fight against Islamic terrorism.

The uprising in Tunisia—called the Jasmine Revolution after a flower native to the region—began with a series of street protests in December 2010. The protests erupted after Mohamed Bouazizi, an educated computer science graduate who sold fruit to support his family, was harassed by police and told to pack up his produce cart. Bouazizi threatened to set himself on fire if the local governor did not meet with him, and he carried out his threat on December 17, 2010. His suicide produced a martyr for millions of Tunisian youth who had become increasingly frustrated with high unemployment, inflation, and a lack of economic opportunities. Young Tunisians also were disgusted with the country's high-level political corruption made especially visible in 2010 in documents released by Wikileaks, an organization that posts often-secret government information online.

Riots first erupted in Sidi Bouzid, the city where Bouazizi died, organized largely by young Tunisians through Internet sites like Twitter and Facebook. Quickly, however, the protests spread throughout the country and gained support from labor unions, lawyer groups, and others. The government responded to the unrest with a police crackdown that included beatings and over a hundred deaths, but the unrest continued unabated. President Ben Ali alternately criticized and sought to appease the demonstrators, ordering a government shake-up, closing schools and universities, and promising more jobs. Ultimately, however, he was forced out of office. On January 14, 2011, President Ben Ali dissolved his government, declared a state of emergency, and fled to Saudi Arabia.

Following the president's departure, a temporary coalition government was created, promising that elections would be held in sixty days. However, protesters rejected the new government, complaining that it contained members of the RCD, and demonstrations continued. On January 27, 2011, Tunisia's prime minister, Mohammed Ghannouchi, announced that six members of the RCD had resigned from the government, meeting protesters' demands. The next chapter of Tunisia's history must now be written, and commentators are divided about what might happen. As of early 2011, the country appeared to be in a political vacuum, but it is possible that Tunisia will replace its autocratic system with a much more democratic government.

Tunisia's revolution has inspired other political rebellions in the Arab world. Egyptians quickly followed the example of Tunisia, and in February 2011 forced longtime president Hosni Mubarak to resign. As of March 2001, a string of other countries in the region—including Libya, Yemen, Algeria, Bahrain, Morocco, and others—were also seeing antigovernment protests.

Whether Tunisia will succeed in fully embracing democracy is a question that cannot yet be answered, but the idea of democracy does seem to have a broad appeal throughout the developing world. The authors of the viewpoints in the following chapter debate the issue of whether these Arab uprisings were influenced by Iran's green movement.

Iran's Green Movement Inspired Protests in Tunisia and Egypt

Barbara Slavin

Barbara Slavin is a nonresident senior fellow at the Atlantic Council, an organization that promotes constructive US leadership and engagement in international affairs. She is the author of the book, Bitter Friends, Bosom Enemies: Iran, the U.S., and the Twisted Path to Confrontation.

While the world's attention has been riveted by Arab uprisings in Tunisia and Egypt this month [January 2011], Iran's government has taken the opportunity to execute a record number of prisoners in an apparent bid to head off the return of the dramatic street protests that pushed President Mahmoud Ahmadinejad's government to the brink in June 2009.

Meanwhile, Iranian officials have been spinning the turmoil in the Arab world as a victory for Iran and a replay of Iran's 1979 revolution against the U.S.-backed shah [Iran's former king]. But the mass protests that are ricocheting around the region—spread in part by Facebook, Twitter, text messaging, and satellite television—cut more than one way for Tehran [Iran's capital]. They remind Iranians of their own recent failed attempt to dislodge an increasingly authoritarian government.

"This is a reaction to the developments in Egypt and Tunisia," says Hadi Ghaemi, director of International Campaign for Human Rights in Iran. "The Iranian intelligence forces want to show their power by executing so many people, including even someone of European nationality."

The crackdown could be in part an effort to pre-empt more demonstrations as Iran on Jan. 31 begins the commemoration of the 32nd anniversary of the Islamic Revolution. The climax of the so-called "10 days of dawn" that began with Ayatollah Ruhollah Khomeini's return from exile in 1979 is Feb. 11, the day the shah's last government fell. Last year, Iran also made a point of executing several political prisoners before that date.

[Iran's spate of political executions] is a reaction to the developments in Egypt and Tunisia.

Executions and Political Prisoners

This January, Ghaemi said, the Iranian government executed 83 people, including on Jan. 29 the first dual national deliberately killed in years: an Iranian-Dutch woman, Zahra Bahrami.

Bahrami, 45, was arrested in December 2009 when Iran's opposition Green Movement took to the streets during the Shiite Muslim holiday of Ashura. She was later accused of trafficking cocaine, a charge that her family asserts was fabricated. In response to her hanging, the Dutch government suspended diplomatic relations with Iran.

According to Ghaemi, Iran executed almost as many people in January 2011 as it did in all of 2005. Since Ahmadinejad replaced Mohammad Khatami in August 2005, the number of executions has risen steadily and now is the highest in the world per capita and second only to China in absolute terms. At least 250 people were executed last year, Ghaemi said, with perhaps another 100 put to death more quietly. In the eastern city of Mashhad near the Afghan border, he said, about 600 people are currently on death row.

Iran also has the dubious distinction of holding the world's oldest known political prisoner: Ebrahim Yazdi, 80, a former foreign minister who has suffered from high blood pressure and prostate cancer and underwent open-heart surgery shortly before his arrest in October. He is due to go on trial on unspecified charges in March [2011]. According to Ghaemi, another 500 political detainees are awaiting action on their cases while about 500 have been convicted and are serving sentences.

Iranian opposition figures point out the regime's hypocrisy in criticizing Arab governments for firing on peaceful protesters while crushing freedom of expression in Iran. Meanwhile, the official media waxes triumphant about the developments in the Arab Middle East.

Comments last week by Hossein Shariatmadari, editor of the conservative *Kayhan* newspaper, were typical: "Look at the region. Tunisia, Egypt, Jordan, Algeria, Bahrain . . . roaring in populous slogans and demands against their absolutist rulers; pay attention. All the demands and slogans are in complete congruence with the teachings of the Islamic revolution. Death to America; death to Israel; hail Islam; death to the seculars; Islam is my religion".

In fact, the demonstrations so far have been largely secular, though well-organized groups such as Egypt's Muslim Brotherhood might become more influential as political transitions move forward—and Tunisia's exiled Islamic leader, Rachid Ghannouchi, returned Jan. 30 to a hero's welcome by thousands of sympathizers.

Iranian Dominance

Clearly, Iran has benefited from events that predate the current upheavals, especially the U.S. toppling of [Iraqi dictator] Saddam Hussein in 2003.

"Iran has had a great string of successes thanks to us," says Chas Freeman, a former U.S. ambassador to Saudi Arabia and veteran Middle East analyst. "Iran is the dominant player in Iraq; its alliance with Syria has been consolidated; its hold on

Lebanese politics now transcends its connection with Syria; and we've shoved a Sunni Salafi group, Hamas, into its arms" (by rejecting Hamas's 2006 electoral victory over Fatah, the secular Palestinian party).

Watching Hosni Mubarak's nearly 30-year presidency twist in the wind is also giving Iran "a great deal of schadenfreude [joy at another's misfortune]," Freeman says, noting the Egyptian leader's long hostility toward Tehran and vice versa.

Iran's Green Movement asserts that [the Arab revolts] . . . were in part inspired by the mass opposition to Iran's 2009 rigged elections.

At the same time, Freeman cautions against connecting what remain disparate dots, noting differences between Muslim countries and uncertainty about their future political trajectories.

"Iran is not a model for anybody not even in Afghanistan or Iraq," he said. "Iranians are trying to use these upheavals, but they don't have a connection to the Iranian revolution, its ideology, or to skillful Iranian diplomacy."

Inspired by the Green Movement

While Iranian state media link the Arab revolts to the 1979 revolution, Iran's Green Movement asserts that they were in part inspired by the mass opposition to Iran's 2009 rigged elections.

In a statement posted Jan. 29 on Facebook, Mir Hossein Mousavi, who challenged incumbent Ahmadinejad in that election, wrote that "the starting point of what we are now witnessing on the streets of Tunis, Sanaa, Cairo, Alexandria, and Suez can be undoubtedly traced back to the days of 15th, 18th and 20th June 2009 when people took to the streets of Tehran in millions shouting 'Where is my vote?' and peacefully demanded to get back their denied rights."

Mousavi noted that the "collapsing political regimes in the Arab world" have also resorted to shutting down the Internet, cell phones, and social networks in an attempt to squelch political change. "Perhaps, they do not realize that continuing policies of intimidation will eventually turn against itself," he wrote in a clear reference to Iran as well as Arab despots. "Pharaohs usually hear the voice of the nation when it is too late."

The Protests in Tunisia and Egypt Are Victories for Iran's Green Movement

Hamid Dabashi

Hamid Dabashi is a professor of Iranian studies and comparative literature at Columbia University in New York.

The democratic Sirocco [a North African wind] that is blowing beautifully eastward from North Africa has refreshing ripples and smells of beautiful jasmine [a reference to Tunisia's so-called Jasmine Revolution] across the River Nile, towards the Persian Gulf, beyond the Arabian Sea, over the Indian Ocean and right into the farthest reaches of Iran and Afghanistan and then right into Central Asia.

The triumph of the democratic will of the Tunisians—and now Egyptians—is a simultaneous victory for the identical aspirations of Iranians who did precisely what we are witnessing in Tunisia and Egypt a year and a half earlier and yet failed to reach for the dream-like finale.

Iranians in and out of their homeland are taking a vicarious delight in the swift success of the Tunisian uprising and in the heroic determinism of Egyptians. Though they have yet to dislodge a far more vicious and entrenched dictatorship that has destroyed their land and distorted their culture for three decades, they are following with punctilious attention the details of the dramatic unfolding of events in Tunisia and Egypt.

In Facebook and Tweets, in websites and webcasts, internet forums and transnational news portals, email list-serves and text messaging—in Persian, French, English, and Arabic, Iranians from around the globe post and repost, watch and re-watch the YouTube clips and [Arab newswire] Al Jazeera streams, following the unfolding events, offering advice, soliciting details, congratulating their Tunisian and Egyptian friends and colleagues, and have already come up with moving posters and graphics uniting their fates—"The future is ours" reads one in Persian, Arabic, and English.

Revolutionary Fervour

This delight need not be only vicarious. There is every real reason for Iranians to partake in the joy and delight of their Tunisian and Egyptian brothers and sisters, for the spread of the Jasmine Revolution is a solid victory for the Green Movement in very precise and measured ways. This wind of freedom knows no colonially manufactured or racialized demarcation. The root causes of these uprisings are the same—from Afghanistan and Iran to Iraq and Palestine, Tunisia and now, the biggest apple of all—the apple whose fall will create a new Newtonian law of plenary motion about us: Egypt! The root cause of these uprisings is a defiance of a politics of despair, an economics of corruption and cruelty.

> *The spread of the Jasmine Revolution [in Tunisia] is a solid victory for the Green Movement [in Iran] in very precise and measured ways.*

It is imperative that the events in Tunisia and Egypt not be assimilated backward into a blind retrieval and habitual regurgitation of Arab nationalism, tempting as the cliché of "Arab Spring" seems to be these days. It is not merely as "Arabs" that Tunisians rose against tyranny. It is not just as "Arabs" that Egyptians have revolted against corrupt government.

It is as citizens of betrayed republics that have been denied them since the end of European colonialism that Tunisians and Egyptians, Yemenis and perhaps others in the region, are rising against the tyrants that rule them—and the US and European interests that keep those tyrants in power against the will of their own people. The commencement of that postcolonial buildup of nations is a deferred promise to all those in the extended shadows of European colonialism, and not just the Arab world. Abusing the memory of the colonial history, traumatised in the US-sponsored coup of 1953, is the very raison d'être of the Islamic Republic, and the brutish theocracy has long since lost it.

The will of the people in Tunisia and Egypt and perhaps the rest of the Arab world is denying the Islamic Republic its insatiable appetite for enemies.

Losing Enemies

The Tunisian and Egyptian victories are victories for the Green Movement in Iran because it is not just the US heavy-handed presence that is deeply troubled by the prospect of losing its chief allies in the region; but the Islamic Republic's opportunism too is losing its major enemies—and in this region losing enemies is worse than losing friends. Over the entirety of its life span, the Islamic Republic has been the singular beneficiary of the politics of despair that has ruled the region, with the pains of Palestine as the epicentre of that opportunism.

The ruling banality in the Islamic Republic has been and remains the direct beneficiary of every catastrophe that befalls the Arab and Muslim world, from Palestine and Lebanon to Iraq and Afghanistan. There is a balance of terror in the region between the US and its regional allies on one side and the Islamic Republic and its sub-national allies ([Palestinian party] Hamas, [Lebanese militant group] Hezbollah, and [Iraq's Sunni] Mahdi Army) on the other. Any change in that balance is not just potentially damaging to the US but even more so to the Islamic Republic—and that is good for the cause of liberty in Iran, and in the region. The will of the people in Tunisia and Egypt and perhaps the rest of the Arab world is denying the Islamic Republic its insatiable appetite for enemies. . . .

In denying the Islamic Republic its insatiable needs for enemies, and in exposing the banality of the assumption that without US aid and neoliberal economics there is no democracy—the spread of the Jasmine Revolution is also a solid victory for the Green Movement.

Egypt's Political Unrest Offers Lessons for Iran's Green Movement

Muhammad Sahimi

Muhammad Sahimi is a political columnist for the Tehran Bureau of the Public Broadcasting Service (PBS), a publicly funded news service based in the United States. He is also a professor of chemical engineering and materials science at the University of Southern California and has written about Iran's nuclear program for many years.

The revolution in Tunisia is spreading to the rest of the Arab world. But it would be a grave mistake to confuse Tunisia with Egypt. Egypt is the most important pillar of American policy in the Middle East, where the United States has been trying to keep together a coalition for its so-called war on terrorism. Egypt is also the most important Arab and Islamic country to have signed a peace agreement with Israel, and the two countries have collaborated to restrict the Palestinian movement Hamas in the Gaza Strip. So, it is not just America that is following the developments in Egypt. Israel too is watching nervously what is happening there, as is the rest of the Middle East. . . .

Lessons for Iran

There are already a few lessons for Iran and its democratic Green Movement. To learn the lessons, we must first understand the similarities and differences between Iran and Egypt, in order to avoid unfounded generalizations from one to the other.

Similarities Between Egypt and Iran

So, what are the similarities between Egypt and Iran?

In both nations, and unlike in Tunisia, the military backs the regimes. The Islamic Revolutionary Guard Corps in Iran wields vast military, economic, and security power. Its high command, led by Major General Mohammad Ali Jafari and Brigadier General Yadollah Javani, head of the Guards' political directorate, supports [Iranian supreme leader] Ayatollah Sayyed Ali Khamenei and [president] Mahmoud Ahmadinejad. Likewise, the regime of [Egyptian president] Hosni Mubarak, a former air force general who has held power since 1981, is supported by Egypt's military. In addition, similar to Iran, Egypt has a vast apparatus for internal security with up to one million personnel.

In both [Egypt and Iran], the Islamic opposition is strong.

In both nations, the share of the population that lives in poverty is high: 50 percent in Egypt, 30–40 percent in Iran. The vast armies of the unemployed youth thus play important roles as citizens strive for political systems responsive to the needs of the people. Egypt's demonstrations appear to be driven by the poor. In Iran, on the other hand, the regime has long succeeded in co-opting the poor. The elimination of subsidies, however, whose severest shock waves are expected to arrive this spring and summer [2011], may change that.

Strong Islamic Opposition

In both nations, the Islamic opposition is strong. Iran's Green Movement is led by devout Muslims, Mir Hossein Mousavi and his wife, Dr. Zahra Rahnavard, Mehdi Karroubi, and former President Mohammad Khatami. For now, there is no alternative to their leadership inside Iran. In Egypt, the Muslim Brotherhood has been the most formidable opposition group to Mubarak's regime. In the parliamentary elections of

2005, the Brotherhood's candidates ran as independents because their party had been declared illegal. They still won 88 seats, 20 percent of the total, which enabled the Brotherhood to form the largest opposition bloc. The Muslim Brotherhood scored this impressive victory in an electoral process that was marred by many irregularities and resulted in the arrests of hundreds of the group's members.

At first the Muslim Brotherhood remained formally aloof from the protests. But quickly recognizing the depth of the people's anger, the group has tried to align itself with the youthful and apparently secular demonstrators, declaring that it would support the protests. The full role of the Muslim Brotherhood in the demonstrations is not yet clear. As in Iran, the protests seem to be spearheaded by angry young people from a cross-section of the country. Robert Fisk of the [British newspaper the] *Independent* reported that the movement is nationalist rather than Islamic, but Egyptian authorities have arrested at least eight top officials of the Muslim Brotherhood and blamed them for the unrest.

Influence of Fiscal Policies

In Egypt, the fiscal policies that the International Monetary Fund (IMF) and the World Bank have dictated to the government—a neoliberal program promoting the free market, devaluation of currency, and elimination of subsidies for basic commodities—have resulted in economic growth, but the gap between the haves and have-nots has widened substantially. Make no mistake. Elimination of subsidies in Iran is exactly the same sort of policy, except that the Ahmadinejad administration has not devalued Iran's rial, because the cheap dollar is used by the Mafia-like groups that are linked with the hardliners to flood Iran with imports from the far East and enrich themselves. All the people that I have been talking to inside Iran tell me that the shock of the hyperinflation that will result from the subsidy cuts will arrive by this summer.

Trade Unions

Unlike in Tunisia, Egypt's trade unions are controlled by the government. In fact, there have been reports that union leaders have called on their members not to participate in the demonstrations, although it is not yet clear whether they have been heeded by the rank and file. Likewise, in Iran [while] the government does not allow true labor unions to become strong and establish organic links with each other, it has also formed "yellow unions" that represent the government's, rather than labor's, interests. In every plant there is a Muslim Association. Most plants, as well as government branches and offices, also have a Basij "resistance base" that monitors what goes on. True labor union leaders, such as Mansour Osanloo, president of the Executive Committee of the Syndicate of Workers of Tehran and Suburbs Bus Company, are in jail.

> *Both nations are strategically important. But whereas Egypt is an ally of the United States and Israel, the Islamic Republic is a foe.*

And in both nations, elections are meaningless. In Egypt, the ruling National Democratic Party "wins" elections because the government bans true opposition parties from participating. Even when it allows some of their members to run, it harasses them and their campaigns. Likewise, in Iran the Guardian Council vets the candidates and disqualifies most of those who oppose the regime from running, nullifies the results of elections that are not to its liking, and supports outright fraud.

Differences Between Egypt and Iran

But there are also significant differences between the two nations and their democratic movements.

Both nations are strategically important. But whereas Egypt is an ally of the United States and Israel, the Islamic Republic is a foe. In addition to its size and large population, Egypt controls the Suez Canal, has diplomatic relations with Israel, and is the staunchest U.S. ally in the Arab world. The [Barack] Obama administration has paid no more than lip service to the cause of democracy in Egypt. In a revealing interview with *Al Jazeera*, State Department spokesman P.J. Crowley seemed to imply that the United States does not support the desire of the Egyptian people to move toward democracy because of Egypt's role in regional "stability." WikiLeaks has released a collection of cables that detail the widespread repression of dissidents by Mubarak's regime. They reveal that the White House has been fully aware of his brutality. While the Obama administration insists that it has been pushing for reforms, the cables reveal that this is not the case, and that even broaching the brutality used against the opposition is a touchy matter. In short, the United States has a vested interested in preserving the regime in Egypt, with or without Mubarak. This should be a lesson to those in the opposition who believe that the United States can help them bring "democracy" to Iran.

Egyptian Regime Is Secular

And, whereas Mubarak's regime is strongly secular, Iran's is religious, albeit based on a reactionary interpretation of Islamic teachings. This fact should also be a lesson to those in the opposition to the Islamic Republic who think that a secular regime will inevitably lead to democracy (or *is* necessarily democratic).

In Egypt, the secular opposition is out in the open, whereas in Iran the seculars do not play any visible role. Therefore, while it is possible for a secular leader, such as Mohamed El-Baradei, former director-general of the International Atomic Energy Agency and Nobel Peace Laureate, to emerge as a viable leader of the opposition, there is no such possibility in Iran, at least not at this point.

There is another significant difference between the two nations. Mubarak's regime has systematically imprisoned, exiled, or eliminated any viable, charismatic opposition leader. Even ElBaradei has been cautious in his opposition. Up until a few days ago, he spoke of returning to Egypt only when there were real election reforms. In contrast, Iran's opposition leaders are in place. The Green Movement has a recognized leadership, which is supported by a very significant portion of the population.

Egypt does not have access to the roughly $80 billion that Iran earns annually from oil export—controlled, of course, by the hardliners. It relies on tourism, some domestic industries, and $1.5 billion a year in aid that it receives from the United States. If unrest continues, tourism will be threatened.

Lessons for the Green Movement

So, what are the lessons for Iran? In my view, the demonstrations in Egypt will not result in real change unless the military withdraws its support for Mubarak. He just ordered his government to resign, but did not resign himself. He also ordered the military into the streets. The *New York Times* reported that senior Egyptian military commanders cut short a previously scheduled visit to the Pentagon to rush home to Cairo.

The Green Movement must spread to [the poorer] strata of society . . . to become an all-encompassing movement for a better Iran.

Keep in mind that the military in Tunisia played a crucial role in the victory of the revolution there. The same is necessary for Iran. The social base of support for the hardliners is significant but very narrow. They rely on the Revolutionary Guards and Basij to crack down on peaceful demonstrators, arrest members of the opposition, and dictate to the judiciary the jail terms that opposition figures receive. Thus, the open support of the rank and file of the military can play an important role in either pushing back the hardliners and forcing them to take meaningful steps to open up society and improve conditions, or toppling them altogether—not through a military coup that will not lead to democracy, but by creating a situation in which the military leaders recognize that they cannot use the armed forces to put down the democratic movement.

In both Tunisia and Egypt, the poor and the unemployed have played important, perhaps leading, roles in recent developments. Thus, another lesson is that the Green Movement must spread to these strata of society, as well, to become an all-encompassing movement for a better Iran.

Despite the recognition that the military backs Mubarak at this point, the Egyptian opposition has not hesitated to demonstrate. The leaders of the Green Movement should also be prepared and have concrete plans in place for the time when the true effect of the elimination of the subsidies, compounded by the hardliners' corruption and incompetence and the externally imposed sanctions, becomes clear, which could be as early as this summer.

You can be sure that Iran's hardliners are watching what is going on nervously. In his sermon during Friday Prayers yesterday [January 28, 2011], the hardline cleric Ahmad Khatami bemoaned the absence of "Islamic leaders" at the forefront of the developments in Tunisia, Egypt, and other Arab countries. He declared that this is the result of a conspiracy by the Western powers, because in his opinion the people of both Tunisia and Egypt have revolted for their religion. Ahmad Khatami and his ilk still do not understand what is happening.

About ten years ago, after several elections made it clear that the conservatives and hardliners could not win even semi-democratic elections in Iran, Ali Larijani—then head of the national TV and radio network, now Majles speaker—said that there was no need to have the support of the majority in order to rule the Islamic Republic. He pointed specifically to Egypt as an example, observing that Mubarak had the support of the army and only 15–20 percent of the population, yet had remained in power for two decades. The unrest in Egypt demonstrates that such a "theory" is wrong and bankrupt. As Mousavi said in his statement about the developments in Egypt and Tunisia, the ruling elite gets the message of the people when it is too late.

The Situation in Iran Differs from That in Tunisia

Steven Heydemann

Steven Heydemann is vice president of the grant and fellowship program at the US Institute of Peace (USIP), an independent, nonpartisan, national institution established and funded by Congress to help prevent and resolve violent international conflicts and promote post-conflict stability and development. He is a specialist on the comparative politics and political economy of the Middle East.

In Tunisia, a small, homogeneous state on the southern Mediterranean, a popular uprising forced the overthrow of a long-ruling dictator in early 2011. Ruthless repression of mass protests failed. In just one month, Tunisians ousted an entrenched authoritarian regime.

In Iran, a mass uprising that lasted six months was brutally suppressed. The Green Movement of 2009 never became a "Green Revolution." Instead, an entrenched authoritarian regime reasserted its authority. The regime's violent repression succeeded. The opposition was broken, and the regime has since tightened its grip on power.

Four factors help explain the success of mass protests in Tunisia and their failure in Iran.

Role of the Military

First, the most decisive factor was the Tunisian army's refusal to shoot. Its defection signaled a fatal crack in the ruling coalition. On its own, the military's role was probably sufficient to bring about the fall of President Zine al-Abidine Ben Ali. The breakdown of authoritarian regimes has historically been

Steven Heydemann, "Why Tunisia and Not Iran," *The Iran Primer: Power, Politics and U.S. Policy*, January 25, 2011. www.iranprimer.usip.org. Copyright © 2011 by United States Institute of Peace. All rights reserved. Reproduced by permission.

due to splits within a ruling coalition—as in Iran's own revolution in 1979 against the monarchy.

The military is critical to an authoritarian regime's survival, but it is most likely to defect when the costs—whether to the army's reputation, its cohesion, or its ability to shape events later on—are too high to justify its continued loyalty.

Four factors help explain the success of mass protests in Tunisia and their failure in Iran.

In Iran, the military lacked the motive of the Tunisian army. Iran's forces, particularly the Revolutionary Guards, are more invested economically and politically in the power structure, so stood to lose far more than Tunisia's army. As a result, [Iranian capital] Tehran's tools of repression remained intact in the face of popular protests. The massive presence of the Basij paramilitary forces, who are under the Revolutionary Guards' control, gave the theocracy's hardliners a reliable instrument of coercion which it used without hesitation against unarmed and peaceful protestors.

Control of the Economy

Second, in Tunisia, political power and control over the economy had become increasingly concentrated in the hands of the ruling family. Its greed and corruption, excessive even by local standards, alienated social groups that had benefitted from Tunisia's liberal economy and ties to the West. The erosion of support among these critical groups left Ben Ali and his family isolated and vulnerable as protests escalated.

In Tunis [capital of Tunisia], Ben Ali's tight grip on political power amplified his vulnerability. No alternative power centers existed to aid Ben Ali or ensure the government's survival once he fled. In his 23 years in power, Ben Ali had undermined the instruments he might otherwise have relied on to retain his grip on power.

In Tehran, the diffusion of political power and decision-making among multiple institutions provided the flexibility needed to squelch challenges from below. The size and scale of Iran's economy has also made it harder for any individual or clique to dominate opportunities for corruption or rent-seeking, ensuring that a broader range of Iranian social groups has a vested interest in the regime's survival.

And the regime, however it might be viewed in the West, retains significant popular support among some segments of Iranian society, especially the poor and marginal who continue to view it as a source of opportunities, employment, and social benefits.

Ideology and Religion

Third, Tunisia and Iran have different ideological contexts. Tunisian politics were distinctly secular; religion was relegated to the private domain. Iranian politics merged state and mosque, tapping into the legitimacy of Islam.

In Iran, the regime's ability to label the Green Movement an enemy of the Islamic revolution posed a formidable challenge to the movement's leadership. Opposition leaders were forced to affirm their loyalty to the Islamic Republic and their identity as reformers appealing for limited change. Strategically, their decision to brand the Green Movement as the loyal opposition may have been necessary. But asking followers to risk their lives in the name of modest reforms is not a formula likely to generate mass support.

In Tunisia, the regime had long abandoned any clear ideological orientation. In an infamous speech just days before his ouster, Ben Ali acknowledged that the economic and social grievances behind Tunisia's uprising were legitimate. The opposition's goals were also clear and unambiguous—Ben Ali's removal from power. Notably, protests were not driven by an explicit ideology, either secular or Islamist. Indeed, the disparate opposition gave little attention to what might happen if it succeeded.

The Tunisian opposition's disorganization and ideological incoherence may well have worked to its advantage. During his quarter-century rule, Ben Ali had earlier crushed Islamists and repressed dissent, so protestors were not hampered by their association with any known opposition figures. Had the Tunisian opposition been dominated by Islamists, for instance, the army may well have defended the regime. The very effectiveness with which Ben Ali's regime hollowed out political space gave Tunisian protestors advantages that their counterparts in Iran lacked.

Finally, scale may also account for the differences. It may have simply been easier to ignite collective action in a country, such as Tunisia, that is small, homogeneous, and narrowly controlled from a single center than in a country, like Iran, that is large, diverse, and diffusely governed by a fragmented political elite.

The Arab Revolutions in Tunisia and Egypt Transcend the Shortcomings of Iran's Islamic Revolution

Roxane Farmanfarmaian

Roxane Farmanfarmaian is an affiliated lecturer in the politics and international studies department at Cambridge University. She is also a visiting scholar at the Middle East Center of the University of Utah. She lived in Iran during the 1979 revolution and hostage crisis.

Just a short four weeks ago [in January 2011], Iran's Green Movement appeared to be the most vibrant political struggle in the Middle East.

That is the case no more. With the uprising in Tunisia that overthrew long-time dictator Zine el Abedine Ben Ali, and with its spread to the streets of Jordan, Lebanon, Yemen and most spectacularly Egypt, the Arab world is on the march, demanding democracy, human rights and jobs.

Yet, for all the hope and enthusiasm on the ground, the worry, particularly in Washington [DC] and other Western capitals, is that a dark side to this wave of popular outpouring lurks in the possible hijacking of the movement by Islamic fundamentalism. Will the Arab experience not repeat what happened in Iran, when the overthrow of the Shah led to the country's takeover by Ayatollahs, the imposition of sharia [Islamic law], and the loss of hard-gained rights for women?

That certainly has been the line Egyptian President Hosni Mubarak has taken until now—and his excuse for three decades of martial law. His warning that it was either him—or the Muslim Brotherhood [an Islamist group]—was designed to instill fear both at home and abroad. And it is a message that has resonated well with Western concerns, particularly in this age of al-Qaeda extremism and Islamic terrorism.

The "either us or them" argument, however, had an earlier incarnation in a mantra often used by Iran's Shah [king]. In his day, it was not Islamism but communism that struck fear in the Western heart, and that is what he suggested would replace him were he to fall. Ensuring against a Red Iran was the impetus behind the CIA [US Central Intelligence Agency] coup that placed him on the throne in 1953—and guaranteed him US support until the bitter end. As a result, the real story of the Iranian revolution—that it was a highly organised, mosque-based movement that over the course of several years had built up the momentum at last to topple the Shah—was ignored until too late.

Arab Uprisings Are Not Islamist

Looking at the movements in Tunisia, Egypt and Jordan as what they really are—rather than as what they are feared to be—reveals broad-based popular uprisings that do not bear the Islamist organisational or ideational imprint. The Egyptians in the streets, much like presumptive coalition leader, Mohamed ElBaradei and women's rights activist Nawal El Saadawi, all state categorically that what is happening in [the Egyptian cities of] Cairo, Suez and Alexandria has nothing to do with the Muslim Brotherhood. The demonstrations were started by bloggers, social media activists, [Arab newswire] *Al Jazeera* watchers—not by the Brotherhood—which joined the demonstrations three days later. There are no Islamist banners being held up in the streets, no Islamist leaders jumping on soap boxes calling the faithful to jihad [holy war].

In Iran in 1979, there were as many banners bearing Islamic slogans as there were banners calling for the Shah to go. The drumbeat of the demonstrations marked Shia holidays, such as Ashura and Tasua, and followed the 40-day Shia mourning ritual for 'martyrs' killed by the Shah's army. The voices of Ayatollah [Ruhollah] Khomeini and other clerics led the demonstrations through exhortations at Friday prayers. In many demonstrations, the women and the men marched separately—the women shrouded in black, head-to-toe chadors. From the outset, for anyone willing to read it, the writing was on the wall: Iran's revolution was Islamic.

The [Arab] demonstrators have only to look east and see the failure of the Green Movement in post-Revolution Iran to remind themselves of what they do not want.

The Arab demonstrations look nothing like the ones in Iran at that time. In Tunis [capital of Tunisia], Ben Ali fled to Saudi Arabia with no hint that Islamist groups—let alone al-Qaeda imports—had contributed to his ouster. And in Cairo and Amman, [Jordan,] the women and men, boys and girls are marching side-by-side, calling for the right to vote, empowerment and human rights.

For anyone willing to read the message, the writing is on the wall—the Arabs are marching because they wish for transparency, employment and the right to be heard.

These are the voices of people who no longer fear the slogans that, if it's not dictatorship, its Islamic extremism. They, much more than any Western observer, are aware that Islamic extremism, sharia and religious governance are as stifling as any other form of authoritarianism. The demonstrators have only to look east and see the failure of the Green Movement in post-Revolution Iran to remind themselves of what they do not want. Washington too needs to move on and recognise that the Arabs are marching to escape once and for all any such heavy-handedness. Theirs are movements that can withstand Islamism, for what they truly seek is dignity, work and freedom.

CHAPTER 4

What Is the Future of Reform in Iran?

Chapter Preface

Iran's 1979 Islamic revolution put into place a unique type of government called an Islamic republic. It gives ultimate power to a religious figure called the supreme leader, but it also includes a president and a parliament elected by the people. Initially, this combination of democratic and theocratic elements caused significant political discord, as presidents sought to share power with much more conservative religious leaders. In recent years, however, conservative religious hardliners have gained control over both the presidency and the parliament, allowing the supreme leader to become all-powerful and causing Iran's government to become more autocratic and repressive. The green movement is seen as the reaction to this repression.

Iran's constitution places the supreme leader at the core of Iran's government system. He is not elected, but is chosen by a group of leading religious clerics called the Assembly of Experts. Ayatollah Ruhollah Khomeini, the religious cleric who spearheaded the country's Islamic revolution, became the first supreme leader, and he was succeeded by Ayatollah Ali Khamenei, a cleric who was Iran's president from 1981 to 1989. The constitution gives the supreme leader significant powers. He is basically authorized to determine and direct all of the country's domestic and foreign policies. He is the commander in chief of Iran's armed forces; he can hire or fire the head of Iran's judiciary; and he appoints six of the twelve members of the powerful Guardian Council, a body that oversees the activities of the parliament and determines which candidates are qualified to run for public office. The supreme leader also controls Iran's radio and TV networks.

The second highest-ranking official in Iran is the president, according to the nation's constitution. He is head of the executive branch, acts as the country's official spokesperson, and has significant power over economic matters. He appoints a cabinet, called the Council of Ministers, which is charged with helping to run different aspects of the country's business, subject to the approval of the parliament. However, compared with presidents of other countries, the Iranian president's role is quite limited. He does not act as commander in chief of the armed forces or make decisions about security, the nation's defense, or major foreign policy issues. Moreover, anyone who wants to run for president must first be approved by the Guardian Council. Many presidential hopefuls are rejected by the Guardian Council, a process that tends to weed out reformers or persons who might challenge the ruling regime. Currently, Iran's president is Mahmoud Ahmadinejad, a conservative and former mayor of Tehran, Iran's capital city. He became president in 2005 and was reelected in 2009 in an election that generated claims of election fraud and sparked the green movement protests in 2009 and 2010.

Iran's parliament, the Majlis, has two hundred ninety members who are elected by popular vote every four years. The unicameral parliament drafts and passes legislation and approves Iran's budget, but all legislation must also be approved by the conservative Guardian Council to make sure it complies with Islamic values before becoming law. The council exercises this power freely, often rejecting legislation passed by the parliament.

Another body elected by Iranians is the Assembly of Experts, a group of eighty-six religious clerics who serve for eight-year terms. Like other elected positions, however, people who run for the assembly must first be vetted and approved by the Council of Guardians. Once elected, the Assembly of Experts choose the supreme leader, historically a cleric from their own ranks who is then reconfirmed time after time.

Clearly the most powerful body in the Iranian government, however, is the Council of Guardians, which is composed of six jurists appointed by the supreme leader and six chosen by the head of the judiciary and the parliament. Each jurist is elected for a six-year term and terms are phased so that not all seats are up for election at the same time. The constitution gives the Guardian Council the responsibility for interpreting the constitution and determining whether laws passed by the parliament are consistent with Islamic law, called sharia. The council also is charged with vetting everyone who wants to run for elected office—for president, parliament, or the Assembly of Experts. Together, the veto power over legislation and the vetting power give the council great control over any attempts to enact reforms to Iran's government, and reformist attempts to reduce the council's powers have been unsuccessful in the past.

Another body, the Expediency Council, has been gaining power in recent years. Created in 1988 by the supreme leader to mediate disputes between the parliament and the Guardian Council, the Expediency Council now functions as an adviser or assistant to the supreme leader, with supervisory powers over all branches of the government. The council has thirty-four members, appointed by the supreme leader, and is currently headed by former president Ayatollah Ali Akbar Hashemi Rafsanjani. Like the Council of Guardians, it is very conservative and antireform.

The judiciary branch of Iran's government is run by the head of the judiciary, who is appointed by the supreme leader. This means that the judiciary is not independent but acts as the arm of the supreme leader. Although some of the judiciary's duties involve mundane civil and criminal cases, the judiciary's most important job is to enforce Islamic law. There are special revolutionary courts that try crimes that threaten national security or the Islamic regime, and these courts are often used to imprison would-be reformers and shut down newspapers and other publications that advocate reform.

With political power and control over the judiciary and armed forces resting firmly in the hands of the supreme leader and his conservative appointees, the structure of Iran's government is a strong impediment to democratic reform. The challenges facing Iran's reform movement are therefore quite daunting, and many experts are doubtful about its near-term prospects. The authors of the viewpoints in this chapter debate the future of reform in Iran.

Iranians Remain Hopeful of Eventual Reform

Jane Bao

Jane Bao is a researcher at Maclean's, *a weekly Canadian magazine, and a contributor to the* University of Toronto *magazine.*

As huge crowds took to the streets in Tehran [Iran's capital city] last year [2009] to protest disputed presidential election results, OISE [Ontario Institute for Studies in Education] professor Shahrzad Mojab agreed to be a guest on a *CBC* [Canadian Broadcasting Company] radio show with Iran's former queen, on the phone from Morocco.

Mojab had become a political exile shortly after the Iranian Revolution of 1979—the same revolution that had unseated the queen and resulted in the arrest or execution of many female activists. Now the two women were being interviewed about a new revolution in Iran.

For Mojab, the rallies following last year's election brought back memories of her own political activism. In an essay, she wrote that the footage of Iranian women protesting had reignited her sense of personal pride: "The images of young Iranian women battling police or even their sheer presence on streets disrupted the image of 'Muslim' women as passive, homebound and wrapped in her symbol of oppression—the veil."

Optimism Amid Setbacks

Many young Iranians in Canada felt strongly about the importance of last year's election, believing that a significant turning point in their home country was at hand. Students from U of T [University of Toronto], Ryerson University, and

York University rented six buses and took about 200 people to vote at the Iranian embassy in Ottawa [the capital of Canada]. They advertised on campus and went to Khorak Supermarket, a popular Iranian plaza in North York, to invite other members of the community to go with them.

Ahmad Shahroodi, who is working on his master's in civil engineering at U of T, drove to Ottawa to vote with four friends. Like many others, he was shocked when Iranian president Mahmoud Ahmadinejad was declared the victor with 63 per cent of the vote. "[Initially,] Tehran was completely silent. No one knew what to do," said Shahroodi. "The second day, people started talking: 'Let's make an assembly out of all the candidates and recount the votes.' But they rejected the proposal. They opened a few ballot boxes in front of the media . . ."

In the crackdown that followed the peaceful rallies, at least 30 people were killed and more than 1,000 arrested. Some protesters received long prison sentences; others were executed. The opposition called off rallies to mark the first anniversary of the protests after threats and pre-emptive arrests. Despite these setbacks, some U of T students and faculty from Iran say they remain optimistic that the movement for greater freedoms has taken root in the hearts and minds of a newly politicized younger generation.

The younger generation will eventually usher in change in Iran.

Change Takes Time

Significant change will take time, though. Amir Hassanpour, a professor in U of T's Department of Near and Middle Eastern Studies, says the Iranian opposition leader, Mir-Hossein Moussavi, fell short of advocating radical political change. "[Moussavi] had an agenda of sharing power with Ahmadinejad's faction. Even if he had full power in replacing Ahmedinejad, there would have been certain legal reforms—minor changes, less pressure on women in terms of veiling—but no constitutional reform."

Hassanpour is critical of the reformist "green" movement, since it would maintain Iran's theocracy. He advocates replacing the theocracy with a secular and democratic regime, which he believes only Iranians working for change in Iran can achieve. "Many intellectuals in North America are actively engaged in the politics of reforming or 'greening' the theocracy rather than getting rid of it," he says. "In doing so, I think they are acting against the interests of not only Iranians but also people throughout the world who are suffering from religious fundamentalism and theocratic rule."

Ramin Jahanbegloo, a U of T political science professor who was detained in solitary confinement for four months in Iran's Evin prison, believes the younger generation will eventually usher in change in Iran. "They have now more inclination towards ideas like human rights, political accountability, and transparency," he says. "Iran is maybe the only country in the Middle East which has the potential for democracy. It has a young population, but also a highly educated urban population."

Ongoing, non-violent action will be crucial to keep up pressure on the administration, says Shahroodi. Ahmadinejad visited Tehran University this past May. "He didn't announce the visit, he did it quietly," Sharoodi observes. "After a while students saw him, told others, and started protesting. He left. He left quickly. The questions are still alive."

Iran's Green Movement Needs Better Organization and Strategy

Karim Sadjadpour

Karim Sadjadpour is an associate at the Carnegie Endowment for International Peace, a private, nonprofit organization dedicated to advancing cooperation among nations and promoting active international engagement by the United States.

This month [June 2010] marks the one-year anniversary of the contested re-election of hard-line Iranian President Mahmoud Ahmadinejad, which spurred the country's largest popular uprisings since the 1979 Islamic revolution. While the regime gradually succeeded in violently quelling the momentum of the opposition Green Movement, the country's deep internal rifts—both among political elites as well as between government and society—are far from being reconciled.

Continuing Divisions

Among the numerous post-election casualties was the notion of Iran as an "Islamic Republic." As the late Grand Ayatollah Ali Montazeri put it, the regime's brutality towards its own people has rendered it "neither Islamic nor a Republic."

Another casualty was the legitimacy of Supreme Leader Ayatollah Ali Khamenei. For two decades, Khamenei deceptively cultivated an image of an impartial and magnanimous guide, but his defiant public support for Ahmadinejad exposed him as a petty, partisan autocrat. Among the unprecedented slogans of last summer's street protests were thunderous chants of "Khamenei is a murderer, his leadership is void!"

Under Khamenei's leadership, an unholy trinity of nouveau riche Revolutionary Guardsmen [part of Iran's military], hard-line clergymen, and indoctrinated Basij militiamen increasingly wield power. Despite his religious pretensions as a spiritual guide, Khamenei's future rests largely in the hands of the Revolutionary Guards. While opposition to his rule among top clerics in [the Iranian city of] Qom worries Khamenei, opposition within the Revolutionary Guard could be fatal for him.

Grass-Roots Nature a Disadvantage

Despite the government's crisis of legitimacy and endemic mismanagement, the Green Movement—nominally led by opposition presidential candidates Mir Hossein Mousavi and Mehdi Karroubi—faces major obstacles. Their brain trust is either in prison, under virtual house arrest, or unable to communicate freely. They lack organization and strategy.

As protests began last year, the grass-roots nature of the Green Movement was initially thought to be advantageous, given that it could not be easily decapitated. "Thirty years ago people were sheep and Khomeini was their shepherd," a prominent Iranian democratic activist told me. "Today we don't have a shepherd, but the people are no longer sheep."

Despite their strength in numbers however, Mousavi and Karroubi's excessive reliance on street protests is misguided. While their courageous supporters espouse tolerance and practice non-violence, they are overwhelmed by armed government forces who are willing to kill and die to retain power.

Mousavi and Karroubi's Gradualist Approach

If the Green Movement is to mount a serious challenge to the government it must incorporate support from bazaar merchants, workers in major industries, transportation unions, and government workers. Sustained strikes by these groups would bring the country's economy to a halt. This is a tall order, however, given that Iran's labor groups, while deeply discontented, are just as amorphous as the Green Movement itself.

What's more, Mousavi and Karroubi, perhaps chastened in part by the unfulfilled promises and excesses of the Islamic Revolution, are seemingly in no hurry to see abrupt change. Instead, they have pursued a gradualist approach that aims to co-opt and recruit disaffected members of the traditional classes, including clergy and Revolutionary Guardsmen, to the Green Movement.

Iran Needs America as an Adversary

The Green Movement's deliberate approach is complicated by the sense of urgency that the United States, Europe, and especially Israel, feel about the Iranian government's nuclear ambitions. While the role that outside powers like the US can play in affecting political reform in Iran is limited, the [Barack] Obama administration faces two fundamental challenges in its Iran policy.

Whatever becomes of the Green Movement in the short term, . . . their country's centennial quest for a democracy is an idea whose time has come.

First, how do you reach an accommodation with a regime that seemingly needs you as an adversary? While a large majority of Iranians want to make amends with the US, for Iran's hardliners, enmity toward the US has become a central part of the Islamic Republic's identity. "If pro-American tendencies come to power in Iran, we have to say goodbye to everything," conceded Ayatollah Ahmad Jannati, head of the powerful Guardian Council. "After all, anti-Americanism is among the main features of our Islamic state."

The second challenge for the US is to champion human rights and democracy in Iran without compromising the independence of opposition forces. Given the diversity of the Green Movement, there is no clear consensus as to which US policies are most constructive. There is a seemingly universal belief that America should absolutely refrain from military action, condemn the Islamic Republic's human rights abuses, and express moral solidarity with the Iranian people. There is little agreement, however, when it comes to more contentious questions, such as the potential efficacy of targeted sanctions.

The Real Leader of the Revolution

Iran's first post-revolution prime minister, Mehdi Bazargan, reportedly once said that the real leader of the 1979 revolution was not Ayatollah [Ruhollah] Khomeini but rather the Shah [Iran's king], who united diverse groups of people against him. Today, a somewhat similar dynamic exists: the two individuals arguably most responsible for the opposition's resilience are not Mousavi and Karroubi, but Ahmadinejad and Khamenei.

Governmental brutality and intimidation can withstand the march of history for years, but not indefinitely. Whatever becomes of the Green Movement in the short term, millions of courageous Iranian protestors made clear to the world last summer that their country's centennial quest for a democracy is an idea whose time has come.

The Iranian Green Movement Faces Numerous Foes

Azadeh Moaveni

Azadeh Moaveni has reported on Iran for Time *magazine and other publications since 1999. She is the author of the books* Lipstick Jihad: A Memoir of Growing Up Iranian in America *(2006) and* Honeymoon in Tehran: Two Years of Love and Danger in Iran *(2009) and the coauthor of* Iran Awakening: One Woman's Journey to Reclaim Her Life and Country *(2007).*

To the hundreds of thousands of Iranians who aspire to democracy and now regularly pour into the streets to prove it, there is no higher sabotage than their government's nuclear brinkmanship. At virtually every important juncture when the country's opposition movement has commanded the world's attention, the regime has cleverly diverted the news cycle with some terrifying-sounding claim about its nuclear program. That now familiar dynamic is shaping the world's reaction to the news emerging from Iran. With anti-government protesters skirmishing with police in neighborhoods throughout the city, President Mahmoud Ahmadinejad announced that Iran had become a nuclear state. Better to remind the world just what sort of scary, uranium-enriching country stands the risk of being destabilized by its would-be democrats.

Powerful Enemies

The government's well-timed nuclear revelations are not all the country's opposition must contend with. In the eight months that have passed since Iran's post-election protest swelled into a full-fledged uprising, the country's so-called Green Movement has made powerful enemies, from Western pundits to diaspora Iranians [Iranians who live outside of Iran], disapproving Arab states to entire television networks. If Lebanon's short-lived, 2005 "Cedar Revolution" inspired international attention all out of proportion to its heft and potential, then Iran's Green Movement suffers from precisely the opposite problem: It captures headlines only once a month, and in between gets disparaged by an influential cast of critics eager to see it fizzle.

Iranian Americans might seem natural supporters of a movement that would, among other things, make it easier for their grandmothers to come visit without getting whisked off to Homeland Security for interrogation. But diaspora Iranians live in constant dread that opposition groups in exile—monarchists and the Mujaheddin-e Khalgh (MKO) [a group that seeks the overthrow of Iran's Islamic regime]—will step in to exploit and hijack any democratic movement that takes shape in Iran. Though these groups lobby Washington aggressively and present themselves to the West as popular opponents of the Tehran regime, they are viewed by most Iranians as discredited and irrelevant, and in the case of the MKO, freakishly cult-like. Iranian Americans' outright hatred for these groups runs so deep that it often shades their attitude toward the Green Movement. It inclines many prominent diaspora figures to overlook how the opposition has spread throughout the country and to prematurely spell its demise. Iranian-American skeptics of the Green Movement would do better to educate people about the bankruptcy of the exiled opposition, rather than to convince the West that Iran's opposition is over before it started.

The Arab Gulf states also eye the Green Movement warily, nervous about what democratic, economically prosperous Iran might portend for their own future. States like Saudi Arabia,

Qatar, and Kuwait stand to lose significantly should Iran emerge from its self-inflicted isolation.

Their camaraderie with the United States is largely based on a mutual enmity with Iran, and their value to Washington would diminish significantly should a democratic, moderate Iran assume a role in the region commensurate with its size, skilled population, and vast natural resources. Countries like Egypt and Syria are also loath for their restive populations to watch a democratic uprising challenge an unpopular government next door. Just as the Iranian revolution of 1979 inspired Islamic radicalism across the Arab world, a successful Green uprising would also spell trouble for the authoritarian Arab status quo.

[The] Green Movement has made powerful enemies, from Western pundits to diaspora Iranians, disapproving Arab states to entire television networks.

Media Foes

Across the media landscape, the Green Movement faces two intractable foes: Iranian state television, which broadcasts pro-government propaganda masquerading as news, and [Arab newswire] *Al Jazeera*, which often does the same about 30 minutes later. Ever since the 1999 student protests at Tehran University, *Al Jazeera* has either ignored or minimized any popular challenge to the Iranian government. The channel's Tehran bureau chiefs have tended to share with the Iranian regime both political ideology and blood relatives. The coverage has on occasion grown so radical that moderate officials in Tehran have cut off the bureau chief's access for growing "too Bin Ladenist." *Al Jazeera English* has calibrated its coverage of the June election and the protests with more sophistication, but a similar bias still runs through its reporting on Iran. Watching its coverage, you could be forgiven for thinking that the jury is still out on whether the Green Movement is actually an elaborate Israeli-American plot abetted by the Western media. The network would argue that it must make compromises to keep its Tehran bureau open at a time when many media outlets have been shut down altogether. But there's little dignity in distorting the story just to stay on the ground.

Iran's Green opposition will have to contend with its international foes, along with the Iranian government itself, in the weeks and months ahead.

From within the American pundit establishment, Flynt and Hillary Mann Leverett—both former [US] National Security Council staffers—have lined up against the Green Movement from its infancy. In the immediate wake of the June election, they published an op-ed entitled "Ahmadinejad Won, Get Over It," chiding those who questioned how a president who bludgeoned his country's economy might have been re-elected by such an enormous margin. Even now, eight months into the Iranian people's refusal to get over it, the Leveretts are still arguing that pro-Ahmadinejad Iran dwarfs Green-Iran. To that end, they actually cite the government's own estimates of crowd attendance at pro-regime rallies, and argue that the majority of Iranians subscribe to President Mahmoud Ahamdinejad's fundamentalist world-view. In an interview with [Israeli newspaper] *Haaretz*, Mann Leverett claims that Ahmadinejad's Holocaust denial rhetoric wins him great popularity in Iran. In all likelihood the Leveretts have never stepped foot inside the country, because anyone who has spent a day in Iran talking to people about their government's support for groups like [Palestinian militants] Hamas know this couldn't be true. The contemptuous image of Iranians that emerges from the Leveretts' analysis—stupid zealots, eager to suffer sometimes triple-digit inflation for the sake of baiting Israel with hateful Holocaust denial—is disturbing and wrong, if not borderline racist. The couple is now probably the Iranian regime's favorite Americans, after, of course, [former US president] Jimmy Carter.

The world tends to gaze smilingly on vibrant, youth-led democracy movements, but Iran's Green opposition will have to contend with its international foes, along with the Iranian government itself, in the weeks and months ahead.

Other Middle East Revolutions May Energize the Iranian Green Movement

Scott Peterson

Scott Peterson is a staff writer for the Christian Science Monitor, *an US-based international news organization with a website, a weekly magazine, and a daily newspaper.*

Energized by people power revolts in Tunisia and Egypt, the opposition in Iran took to the streets on Monday [February 14, 2011], breaking a spell of fear and intimidation for the first time in more than a year.

Security forces fired tear gas, paintball guns, and bullets into the air, to disperse crowds as tens of thousands of protesting Iranians defied rally bans in Tehran [Iran's capital] and major cities to voice their solidarity with Arab revolts and anger at Iran's hard-line leaders.

Officials had declared the opposition Green Movement a "corpse," while taking every measure to preempt a rekindling of past protests—and lethal street battles—that lasted for weeks after disputed June 2009 elections.

The Green Movement Reinvigorated

The irony wasn't lost on Iran's latent opposition in recent days, as Iran's top leaders claimed to be at the forefront of a popular "Islamic awakening" that was sweeping across the Arab world—but would not allow it to touch Iran.

"The government tried to say this movement is dead, it's a corpse," says an observer in Tehran who could not be named. "But for a corpse, you don't organize maximum security forces all over Tehran. This is the most important point today.... Do [hard-liners] doubt finally? Or still hold the illusion that it's just a few hundred crazy people out there?"

The [Green] Movement ... has, at least in people's hearts and minds, [been given a] great boost of morale and knowing the movement is still there.

"It's not that the number is huge by any standards," adds the observer. "It's huge because there was so much repression during the last year, so these people risking and coming out was beyond expectation."

The fact that there was any turnout at all, after the systematic measures taken against the Green Movement and its leaders since mid-2009—among them executions, rape in detention, and stiff prison sentences—served to invigorate its foot soldiers.

"People will definitely believe in themselves again." says a London-based Iranian analyst who closely monitored events on Monday. "The [Green] Movement showed it still has strength.... It has, at least in people's hearts and minds, [been given a] great boost of morale and knowing the movement is still there."

The scenes on the streets on Monday resembled those of the protests of 2009 against the declared reelection of President Mahmoud Ahmadinejad. Scores, if not hundreds, died and thousands were arrested then. More than 100 were charged with fomenting a "velvet revolution" in a show trial.

"Death to the Dictator"

On Monday cellphone video showed people chanting "Death to the dictator," and linking Iran's supreme religious leader, Ayatollah Ali Khamenei, to ousted Egyptian President Hosni Mubarak.

One poster made for the event showed comparison pictures of Mr. Mubarak and President Ahmadinejad striking the same arms-raised-in-victory pose. That was a note struck by US Secretary of State Hillary Clinton, who called for the Iranian government to recognize the "aspirations" of its people, as it had for Egyptians.

"What we see happening in Iran today is a testament to the courage of the Iranian people and an indictment of the hypocrisy of the Iranian regime, a regime which over the last three weeks has constantly hailed what went on in Egypt," Mrs. Clinton said. "And now, when given the opportunity to afford their people the same rights as they called for on behalf of the Egyptian people, [they] once again illustrate their true nature."

State television dismissed the protesters as "hypocrites, monarchists, thugs, and seditionists who wanted to create public disorder in Iran [and] were arrested by our brave nation. . . . These people set garbage bins on fire and damaged public property."

In one violent episode caught on video, a *basiji* religious militiaman tried to stop a crowd desecrating a banner with a portrait of Ayatollah Khamenei and the founder of Iran's 1979 Islamic Revolution, Ayatollah Ruhollah Khomeini. The *basiji* was viciously kicked and beaten as an agent of the regime.

The government tried to headline news of Turkish President Abdullah Gul's visit to Iran. But Mr. Gul's call for Middle East leaders to hear their people gave Iran's opposition a boost.

"We see that sometimes, when the leaders and heads of countries do not pay attention to the nations' demands, the people themselves take action to achieve their demands," Gul said on Monday during a joint news conference with Ahmadinejad.

Green Movement protests peaked in December 2009, but huge rallies planned for February 2010 were preempted by arrests and saturation deployment of security forces and intelligence agents.

Virtual House Arrest
for Opposition Leaders

Since then opposition leaders—former presidential candidates Mir Hossein Mousavi and Mehdi Karroubi, both of them former senior officials—have been under virtual house arrest and vilified by hard-line officials as traitors.

Before his phone lines were cut off, his house surrounded, and guards placed to prevent visits from anyone, including his children—and to prevent him from attending Monday's demonstration—Mr. Karroubi told *The New York Times* in a Skype interview last week that the event was a test for the Iranian regime.

"If they are not going to allow their own people to protest, it goes against everything they are saying, and all they are doing to welcome the protests in Egypt is fake," said Karroubi.

Prior to Monday's protest, dozens of journalists and activists were detained, though protest routes had already been mapped out in 30 cities and circulated on the Internet.

On Monday, security forces in riot gear—and in some places, according to eyewitnesses, wearing face masks for the first time—deployed in major squares and patrolled the streets in motorcycle posses.

The security forces have "also learned," since 2009, says the London analyst. "They are showing crowd management now, less thug-like and more trained. Still brutal, but dispersing people before a nucleus is formed, funneling [crowds] to keep [people] moving."

Still, he says, the images of Iran's most sacred leadership icons being driven over by cars—even more than video of burning trash bins and clashes—are the ones that will resonate at the top in Iran.

"It took ages to get there [in 2009], but [only] a few hours this time," he says. "It's there, the people do have it in them."

Iran's Green Movement Will Not Rise Up After Protests in Tunisia and Egypt

Hooman Majd

Hooman Majd, an Iranian American writer, is the author of the book The Ayatollahs' Democracy: An Iranian Challenge *(2010).*

There has been a temptation in the West to tie the convulsions in Tunisia, Egypt and elsewhere in the Arab world to Iran's 2009 green movement protests. Those large demonstrations are being cited as the sparks that ignited the imagination of all who live under repressive regimes in the Middle East.

In Tehran, meanwhile, the government has not shied away from reporting the Arab uprisings. But analogies are made not with the fetneh, or sedition, as the 2009 post-election crisis is described. Rather, they are made with the Islamic Revolution of 1979, which swept the shah off the Peacock Throne and into ignominious exile. Shah Mohammad Reza Pahlavi, much like Egypt's President Hosni Mubarak, was a lifetime dictator closely allied with Washington.

This Iranian narrative, however, is far closer to the truth. If there is any secret desire among U.S. officials that Iran's opposition green movement will now be motivated by what it inspired and rise up again to overthrow the Islamic system, those hopes will most likely be dashed.

Facile comparisons aside, Persians are not Arabs and have little in common with them culturally, politically or even religiously. Unlike Arabs, Iranians have a long history, more than a century, of democratic movements. Their struggle since the fall of the shah for representative government has not depended on the removal of one man or one family.

The West's view that Iran has an overwhelmingly unpopular dictatorship and that the green movement sought to overthrow the political system is fundamentally wrong.

Both before and after the contested 2009 election, Iran has been more politically analogous to the red state, blue state dynamic in the United States than to the one-man rule of many Arab states. The media, indeed, had focused on protesters and demonstrators in 2009 and on the government's heavy crackdown. It largely ignored, however, the extent of support that President Mahmoud Ahmadinejad did have—which even green movement leaders estimated to be in the millions. Support for the supreme leader and the Islamic system was, and is, far greater.

In the almost two years since, Iranian exiles and many Western analysts have declared the country an unredeemable dictatorship. But within Iran, citizens see politics as usual: continuing disputes, challenges and debate among the three branches of government—with Ahmadinejad not always coming out on top.

That is not to say that there is no discontent or that the green movement—more a civil rights movement than the revolution that many in the West had hoped for—is completely irrelevant. But, until now, Arab protesters could have only dreamed about what Iran has achieved politically in the past 30-plus years.

Arab countries have also had dictators who were supported, coddled and encouraged by Washington and who acted against the wishes of their citizens. But Iran has been free of foreign influence—even if its citizens haven't always agreed with the government's policies.

Iran has been subjected to U.S. sanctions, which affect ordinary citizens' quality of life, while Arab countries are key strategic allies and their governments receive billions of dollars in U.S. support—little of which trickles down to their citizens.

It may be a stretch for the Iranian government to proclaim that Arab protesters are revolting against U.S. hegemony as much as they are against dictatorship. But it is indisputable that the popular opinion of Arab states runs contrary to what we ordinarily call "U.S. interests."

It is not so different in Iran—except that popular opinion on U.S. interests, at least among the majority of Iranians, is in line with the government's. That's not to say that the anti-Americanism displayed by Iranians is anything but anti-imperialism, and Iran's youth are, famously, the most pro-American—but not pro-U.S. foreign policy—in the region.

One reason the green movement lost steam in Iran, however, and is unlikely to reappear anytime soon, apart from the severity of the government's crackdown, is that the government has been successful in portraying itself—at least to moderate supporters—as being aligned with Western interests.

The green movement's large number of demonstrators gave the impression that the entire country was unified behind one goal. But . . . that turned out to be an illusion.

I was in Tehran when the Tunisian president fled his country and after the Hezbollah-engineered collapse of the Lebanese government. The Iranian media covered both extensively. But there was little indication that Iran's youth were readying themselves for another challenge to authority.

In the West, Iranian supporters of the green movement were quick to disseminate catchy slogans: "Tunes tunest, Iran natunest," meaning Tunisia could, Iran couldn't or, better yet, "Tunis envy." Certainly there may be Iranians who are envious of the ease with which the Arabs dispatched their leader. But

Iran's green movement had more in common with the Lebanese Cedar Revolution of 2005 than with the 2011 uprising in North Africa.

As with the Lebanese protests, the green movement's large number of demonstrators gave the impression that the entire country was unified behind one goal. But again, much like the Cedar Revolution, that turned out to be an illusion.

Many of the green movement's demands still resonate with Iranians—some even, evidently, with Ahmadinejad and his government. But major change in Iran is unlikely to come about through street protests—which is why no one calls for them anymore. Not while the whole country, unlike in the Arab states, isn't united in hatred of its leaders.

Iran's Leaders Are Unlikely to Allow Any Opening for Protest

Daniel Brumberg

Daniel Brumberg is a senior adviser to the Center for Conflict Analysis and Prevention at the US Institute of Peace, an independent, nonpartisan institution established and funded by Congress to help prevent and resolve international conflicts and promote stability and development.

Strategically, Iran is hedging its position on the new Middle East turmoil.

The theocrats like to publicly portray the democratic revolts in Tunisia and Egypt as an Islamist tsunami sweeping away corrupt autocracies to replace them with Islamic regimes. But the same leaders are also nervous about doing or saying anything that might, in turn, encourage Iran's own opposition movements.

Supreme Leader Ayatollah Ali Khamanei heralded Egypt's "Islamic awakening. The Egyptian nation has achieved great honors in the path of Islamic struggle and promoting innovative Islamic thoughts," he said. "There is no doubt that this nation will not tolerate the treachery of its leaders and will confront them."

The supreme leader also cautioned, however, that Iran would not "get engaged and wake up a nation such as the Egyptian nation to its duties."

The Iranian Regime's Fears

Tehran [Iran's capital] appears to be as concerned that Egypt's popular rebellion echoes—and might even inspire—Iran's opposition Green Movement. Iran witnessed mass protests that lasted six months in 2009 before they were quashed. The theocrats may see more similarities between Egypt and Iran's 2009 revolt than the Islamic revolution of 1979.

The leaders of Iran's Green Movement have been thinking along the same lines. Opposition leader Mir Hossein Mousavi made the analogy. "Today the slogan of 'Where is my vote?' of the Iranian people is echoed in the slogan of 'The people demand the overthrow of the regime' in [Egyptian cities] Cairo, Suez, and Alexandria," he said.

For the [Iranian] theocrats, any negotiation with the opposition would undermine the ideological purity of the revolution.

Iran's opposition has even demanded that its supporters get the same right to peacefully protest that Egyptians have gained since January 25 [2011]. Its admonitions have exposed the deep contradictions behind the regime's support for Egypt's democratic movement.

Differences Between the Movements

But there are also significant differences between the Iranian and Egyptian opposition movements that explain why Egypt's protestors may achieve more success than their Iranian counterparts.

The core difference is in the ideology and political divide between the regime and the opposition. Iran is an Islamist regime. Its attempts to impose rigid religious dogma have provoked a backlash particularly among the young, who have called in large numbers for democracy and a state that does not force feed religion—both threats to the Islamic Republic's identity. For the theocrats, any negotiation with the opposition would undermine the ideological purity of the revolution.

Egypt, by contrast, has a largely secular government without a central ideology. Its rulers have long governed through a mix of nationalism, Arabism, hobbled state-managed pluralism and state-managed (and at times promoted) Islamism. Its ruling class is also fragmented in ways that open up space for a negotiated transition. And Egypt's army differs in many ways from Iran's Revolutionary Guard [a branch of Iran's military] and paramilitary Basij [an Iranian militia group]. The latter two groups see themselves as defenders of ideological orthodoxy, whereas Egypt's army espouses a more pragmatic, nationalist ethos that is not necessarily adverse to some of the popular demands advanced by Egypt's protestors.

Islamists are important actors in Egyptian politics and society, but secularists, nationalists, labor activists and others are equally important. And ten percent of the population is Christian. Egypt's Islamists may emerge as the strongest opposition force, but what they seek is influence over national policy—particularly in the educational, legal and moral spheres—rather than direct rule. In contrast to Iran's leaders, who espouse an interpretation of Shi'ite Islam that places ultimate authority in the clergy, Egypt's Sunni Muslim Brethren are largely lay political activists. While they want Islam to have a role in public life, they do not want to create an Iranian-style theocracy.

The significant differences between Egypt and Iran make it unlikely that Iran's leaders will tolerate any kind of political opening in the near future.

Iran Unlikely to Allow Uprising

Although Iran has claimed partial credit for Egypt's uprising, the political outcome in Cairo may actually be discomforting for Tehran. The Egyptian opposition has called for democracy that provides participation, representation and pluralism. The

Muslim Brotherhood has even urged "civil rule" and said it will not run a presidential candidate.

Moreover, the United States and its allies in the West could even get credit for helping facilitate the transfer of power. And any new government in Cairo is likely to continue to have relations with Washington, even if they are not as close.

The significant differences between Egypt and Iran make it unlikely that Iran's leaders will tolerate any kind of political opening in the near future. Indeed, even as Iran's leaders applaud the "Muslim masses" and bless Egypt's uprising as a harbinger of Islamic revolution in the entire region, they rejected the Green Movement's request to hold a march to show solidarity with "the freedom-seeking movement embarked on by Tunisian and Egyptian people against their autocratic governments."

The Iranian Green Movement Must Operate on Its Own Timetable

Mohsen Milani, interviewed by World Blog

Mohsen Milani is chair of the government and international affairs department at the University of South Florida. MSNBC .com is a news website owned and operated as a joint venture by NBCUniversal and Microsoft.

Clashes between Iranian police and tens of thousands of protesters erupted in central Tehran [Iran's capital city] on Monday [February 14, 2011,] as security forces beat and fired tear gas at opposition supporters hoping to evoke Egypt's recent popular uprising. The opposition—the "Green Movement," which held months of protests after Iran's disputed 2009 presidential elections—called for the demonstration in solidarity with Egypt's popular revolt, which forced the country's president to resign last week after nearly 30 years in office. The rally is the first major show of strength for Iran's cowed opposition in more than a year.

MSNBC.com invited Mohsen Milani, professor of politics and chair of the Department of Government and International Affairs at the University of South Florida in Tampa, Fla., to respond to questions about the renewed demonstrations by the Iranian opposition and the impact of Egypt's protests on the region. Milani has written extensively about Iran's foreign and security policies, the Persian Gulf, and Iran's revolution of 1979.

[MSNBC.com:] *What are you hearing about what is happening in Iran today?*

[Mohsen Milani:] So far, there are conflicting reports about the size of the pro-democracy demonstrations in Tehran and other cities. It appears that there were no large pro-democracy demonstrations, as some people had hoped for. My impression is that there were small gatherings of protesters here and there, but the police and the security forces were conspicuously present and were determined to contain the gatherings.

Are you surprised that the protesters took to the streets despite the government telling them not to demonstrate?

The "Green Movement" has to operate based on its own clock and must determine its own tempo depending on the conditions in Iran.

Not really. Immediately after the disputed June presidential election in Iran in 2009, millions of Iranians took to the street of the country's major cities, asking, "Where is my vote?" While it is true that Iran's security forces crushed the June uprising, they have been unable to eradicate the roots of discontent, particularly among Iran's highly educated, restless and computer-savvy young generation. The opponents of the Islamic Republic are looking for every opportunity to publicly express their dissatisfaction, and they thought that the Cairo [Egypt's capital city] uprising had created a favorable international atmosphere to revitalize their movement. But when they publicly announce their plans for demonstrations and even publicize the routes for their marches, they should not have expected that Iran's highly effective security forces would allow them to assemble in large numbers.

What does this mean for the future of the opposition movement in Iran?

The planned demonstrations today were ostensibly in support of the uprising in Egypt. The "Green Movement" has to operate based on its own clock and must determine its own tempo depending on the conditions in Iran, and not on what is happening in Cairo or elsewhere. Tehran is not Cairo, and the Islamic Republic is not [former Egyptian president Hosni] Mubarak's regime. While the U.S. enjoyed limited influence to persuade Mubarak and the Egyptian armed forces not to rely on brute force, it has no such leverage with the Islamic Republic. This is why the pro-American regimes in the region are somewhat more vulnerable to this new wave of democracy.

Are members of the opposition in Iran in contact with protest organizers/youth movement in Egypt?

Based on Monday's report in *The New York Times*, there were some contacts between the youth movements of the two countries.

Do you think what happened in Egypt will impact the rest of the region?

Yes, I do. What happened in Egypt in those eighteen days was an inspiring, momentous, authentic and heroic movement to promote democracy. It was a dignified and popular uprising that started with the youth and captured the world's imagination, and proved that it is possible for the people to overthrow a well-entrenched regime through peaceful means. Egyptians from all walks of life and from all ideological persuasions were united in demanding an end to Mubarak's corrupt and authoritarian rule—a regime that deprived the people of their basic human rights and brutally suppressed all voices of dissent. Every president-for-life, king, demagogic leader and theocrat in the Middle East and beyond is probably feeling vulnerable and nervous now. And that is good. The people in Jordan, Yemen, Bahrain and Algeria are demanding meaningful changes from their leaders. In the medium and long term, however, the impact of the Egyptian uprising is not that clear. If democracy develops in Egypt, or if some kind of representative, parliamentary system is established there, then Egypt could become the harbinger of a much-needed democratic order in that troubled region. On the other hand, if chaos prevails in Egypt, or if the military reestablishes its rule and imposes "Mubarakism without Mubarak," then all democratic forces in the region will suffer. We can say that a new chapter has indeed been opened in the region's history, but the pages and the conclusions of it will be written in the coming years.

The United States Must Stop Obstructing Iran's Pro-democracy Movement

Chris Hedges

Chris Hedges is a columnist for Truthdig, an online news source. He spent nearly two decades as a foreign correspondent in Central America, the Middle East, Africa, and the Balkans, reporting for National Public Radio, the Christian Science Monitor, Dallas Morning News, *and* New York Times.

Iranians do not need or want us to teach them about liberty and representative government. They have long embodied this struggle. It is we who need to be taught. It was Washington that orchestrated the 1953 coup to topple Iran's democratically elected government, the first in the Middle East, and install the compliant shah [king] in power. It was Washington that forced [Iranian] Prime Minister Mohammed Mossadegh, a man who cared as much for his country as he did for the rule of law and democracy, to spend the rest of his life under house arrest. We gave to the Iranian people the corrupt regime of the shah and his savage secret police and the primitive clerics that rose out of the swamp of the dictator's Iran. Iranians know they once had a democracy until we took it away.

A Corrupt US Mideast Policy

The fundamental problem in the Middle East is not a degenerate and corrupt Islam. The fundamental problem is a degenerate and corrupt Christendom. We have not brought freedom and democracy and enlightenment to the Muslim world. We have brought the opposite. We have used the iron fist of the American military to implant our oil companies in Iraq, occupy Afghanistan and ensure that the region is submissive and cowed. We have supported a government in Israel that has carried out egregious war crimes in Lebanon and Gaza and is daily stealing ever greater portions of Palestinian land. We have established a network of military bases, some the size of small cities, in Iraq, Afghanistan, Saudi Arabia, Turkey and Kuwait, and we have secured basing rights in the Gulf states of Bahrain, Qatar, Oman and the United Arab Emirates. We have expanded our military operations to Uzbekistan, Pakistan, Kyrgyzstan, Tajikistan, Egypt, Algeria and Yemen. And no one naively believes, except perhaps us, that we have any intention of leaving.

The history of modern Iran is the history of a people battling tyranny. These tyrants were almost always propped up and funded by foreign powers.

We are the biggest problem in the Middle East. We have through our cruelty and violence created and legitimized the Mahmoud Ahmadinejads [Iran's conservative president] and the Osama bin Ladens [al Qaeda leader]. The longer we lurch around the region dropping iron fragmentation bombs and seizing Muslim land the more these monsters, reflections of our own distorted image, will proliferate. The theologian Reinhold Niebuhr wrote, "Perhaps the most significant moral characteristic of a nation is its hypocrisy." But our hypocrisy no longer fools anyone but ourselves. It will ensure our imperial and economic collapse.

Iran's History of Fighting Tyranny

The history of modern Iran is the history of a people battling tyranny. These tyrants were almost always propped up and funded by foreign powers. This suppression and distortion of

141

legitimate democratic movements over the decades resulted in the 1979 revolution that brought the Iranian clerics to power, unleashing another tragic cycle of Iranian resistance. "The central story of Iran over the last 200 years has been national humiliation at the hands of foreign powers who have subjugated and looted the country," Stephen Kinzer, the author of *All the Shah's Men: An American Coup and the Roots of Middle East Terror*, told me. "For a long time the perpetrators were the British and Russians. Beginning in 1953, the United States began taking over that role. In that year, the American and British secret services overthrew an elected government, wiped away Iranian democracy, and set the country on the path to dictatorship."

"Then, in the 1980s, the U.S. sided with Saddam Hussein in the Iran-Iraq war, providing him with military equipment and intelligence that helped make it possible for his army to kill hundreds of thousands of Iranians," Kinzer said. "Given this history, the moral credibility of the U.S. to pose as a promoter of democracy in Iran is close to nil.

"Especially ludicrous is the sight of people in Washington calling for intervention on behalf of democracy in Iran when just last year they were calling for the bombing of Iran. If they had had their way then, many of the brave protesters on the streets of Tehran today—the ones they hold up as heroes of democracy—would be dead now."

US Lack of Credibility

Washington has never recovered from the loss of Iran—something our intelligence services never saw coming. The overthrow of the shah, the humiliation of the embassy hostages, the laborious piecing together of tiny shreds of paper from classified embassy documents to expose America's venal role in thwarting democratic movements in Iran and the region allowed the outside world to see the dark heart of the American empire. Washington has demonized Iran ever since, painting it as an irrational and barbaric country filled with primitive, religious zealots. But Iranians, as these street protests illustrate, have proved in recent years far more courageous in the defense of democracy than most Americans.

Where were we when our election was stolen from us in 2000 by Republican operatives and a Supreme Court that overturned all legal precedent to anoint George W. Bush president? Did tens of thousands of us fill the squares of our major cities and denounce the fraud? Did we mobilize day after day to restore transparency and accountability to our election process? Did we fight back with the same courage and tenacity as the citizens of Iran? Did [2000 presidential candidate] Al Gore defy the power elite and, as [Iranian] opposition candidate Mir Hossein Mousavi has done, demand a recount at the risk of being killed?

The greatest favor we can do for democracy activists in Iran . . . is withdraw our troops from the region.

President [Barack] Obama retreated in his Cairo [Egypt] speech into our spectacular moral nihilism, suggesting that our crimes matched the crimes of Iran, that there is, in his words, "a tumultuous history between us." He went on: "In the middle of the Cold War, the United States played a role in the overthrow of a democratically elected Iranian government. Since the Islamic Revolution, Iran has played a role in acts of hostage-taking and violence against U.S. troops and civilians." It all, he seemed to say, balances out.

I am no friend of the Iranian regime, which helped create and arm Hezbollah [Arab militant Islamist group], is certainly meddling in Iraq, has persecuted human rights activists, gays, women and religious and ethnic minorities, embraces racism and intolerance and uses its power to deny popular will. But I do not remember Iran orchestrating a coup in the United States to replace an elected government with a brutal dictator who for decades persecuted, assassinated and imprisoned democracy activists. I do not remember Iran arming and funding a neighboring state to wage war against our country. Iran never shot down one of our passenger jets as did the USS *Vincennes*—caustically nicknamed Robocruiser by the crews of other American vessels—when in June 1988 it fired missiles at an Airbus filled with Iranian civilians, killing everyone on board. Iran is not sponsoring terrorism within the United States, as our intelligence services currently do in Iran. The attacks on Iranian soil include suicide bombings, kidnappings, beheadings, sabotage and "targeted assassinations" of government officials, scientists and other Iranian leaders. What would we do if the situation was reversed? How would we react if Iran carried out these policies against us?

Standing with the Green Movement

We are, and have long been, the primary engine for radicalism in the Middle East. The greatest favor we can do for democracy activists in Iran, as well as in Iraq, Afghanistan, the [Persian] Gulf and the dictatorships that dot North Africa, is withdraw our troops from the region and begin to speak to Iranians and the rest of the Muslim world in the civilized language of diplomacy, respect and mutual interests. The longer we cling to the doomed doctrine of permanent war the more we give credibility to the extremists who need, indeed yearn for, an enemy that speaks in their crude slogans of nationalist cant and violence. The louder the Israelis and their idiot allies in Washington call for the bombing of Iran to thwart its nuclear ambitions, the happier are the bankrupt clerics who are ordering the beating and murder of demonstrators. We may laugh when crowds supporting Ahmadinejad call us "the Great Satan," but there is a very palpable reality that has informed the terrible algebra of their hatred.

Our intoxication with our military prowess blinds us to all possibilities of hope and mutual cooperation. It was Moham-

med Khatami, the president of Iran from 1997 to 2005—
perhaps the only honorable Middle East leader of our time—
whose refusal to countenance violence by his own supporters
led to the demise of his lofty "civil society" at the hands of
more ruthless, less scrupulous opponents. It was Khatami who
proclaimed that "the death of even one Jew is a crime." And
we sputtered back to this great and civilized man the primitive slogans of all deformed militarists. We were captive, as all
bigots are, to our demons, and could not hear any sound but
our own shouting. It is time to banish these demons. It is
time to stand not with the helmeted goons who beat protesters, not with those in the Pentagon who make endless wars,
but with the unarmed demonstrators in Iran who daily show
us what we must become.

The fight of the Iranian people is our fight. And, perhaps
for the first time, we can match our actions to our ideals. We
have no right under post-Nuremberg laws [enacted after World
War II] to occupy Iraq or Afghanistan. These occupations are
defined by these statutes as criminal "wars of aggression."
They are war crimes. We have no right to use force, including
the state-sponsored terrorism we unleash on Iran, to turn the
Middle East into a private gas station for our large oil companies. We have no right to empower Israel's continuing occupa-
tion of Palestine, a flagrant violation of international law. The
resistance you see in Iran will not end until Iranians, and all
those burdened with repression in the Middle East, free themselves from the tyranny that comes from within and without.
Let us, for once, be on the side of those who share our democratic ideals.

Organizations to Contact

The editors have compiled the following list of organizations concerned with the issues debated in this book. The descriptions are derived from materials provided by the organizations. All have publications or information available for interested readers. The list was compiled on the date of publication of the present volume; names, addresses, phone and fax numbers, and e-mail and Internet addresses may change. Be aware that many organizations take several weeks or longer to respond to inquiries, so allow as much time as possible.

Brookings Institution
1775 Masachusetts Ave. NW, Washington, DC   20036
(202) 797-6000 • fax: (202) 797-6004
e-mail: brookinfo@brook.edu
website: www.brookings.edu

The Brookings Institution is a think tank that conducts research and education in the areas of foreign policy, economics, government, and the social sciences. Its website features numerous briefings and publications on events occurring in Iran. Examples of recent articles include "After Egypt and Tunisia, Is Iran Next?" and "Egypt, Tunisia . . . and Iran."

Century Foundation
1333 H St. NW, 10th Fl., Washington, DC   20005
(202) 387-0400 • fax: (202) 483-9430
website: www.tcf.org

The Century Foundation, founded in 1919 by the progressive businessman Edward A. Filene, is a nonprofit public policy research institution committed to the belief that a mix of effective government, open democracy, and free markets is the most effective solution to the major challenges facing the United States. One of the foundation's projects is a website called InsideIran.org, which is a rich source of information and articles about US-Iran relations, including the article "Is the Sanctions Debate Justifying the Military Option?" and "How Likely Is an Iranian Nuclear Counterstrike?"

Council on Foreign Relations (CFR)

1777 F St. NW, Washington, DC   20006

(202) 509-8400 • fax: (202) 509-8490

website: www.cfr.org

The Council on Foreign Relations is an independent, nonpartisan membership organization, think tank, and publisher. CFR's website is a source of analysis and context on international events and trends. It publishes backgrounders, interviews, "first-take" analysis, expert blogs, and a variety of multimedia offerings. The site also presents books, reports, congressional testimony, and op-eds. In addition, CFR publishes *Foreign Affairs*, a magazine dedicated to serious discussions of American foreign policy and international affairs. Iran is one of the regions that CFR studies, and a search of the website produces numerous articles relevant to reform efforts. Recent articles include "Iranian Re-revolution" and "Letter from Tehran: Iran's New Hardliners."

Heritage Foundation

214 Massachusetts Ave. NE, Washington, DC   20002-4999

(202) 546-4400

website: www.heritage.org

The Heritage Foundation is a research and educational institution—a think tank—whose mission is to formulate and promote conservative public policies based on the principles of free enterprise, limited government, individual freedom, traditional American values, and a strong national defense. The foundation publishes reports, factsheets, testimony, commentaries, articles, and blogs about a variety of domestic and foreign policy matters, including US-Iran relations. A search of the website produces a list of articles and blogs on Iran and its reform movement, including, for example, "U.S. Needs

Stronger Response to Human Rights Violations in Iran" and "With Enemies Like These: Facebook and Twitter Under Iranian Attack."

Institute for Policy Studies (IPS)

1112 Sixteenth St. NW, Ste. 600, Washington, DC   20036
(202) 234-9382
e-mail: info@ips-dc.org
website: www.ips-dc.org

The Institute for Policy Studies is a progressive think tank that focuses on national and international peace, justice, and environmental issues. In order to influence policymakers, the press, the public, and key social movements, IPS fellows and associates publish a wide variety of materials, including books, reports, op-eds, commentaries, fact sheets, talking points, speeches, and event transcripts. Recent reports include "It's Time to Step Up Diplomacy with Iran" and "The United States and the Prospects for Democracy in Islamic Countries."

International Campaign for Human Rights in Iran

Washington, DC
(202) 573-2046
e-mail: rudi@iranhumanrights.org
website: www.iranhumanrights.org

The International Campaign for Human Rights in Iran was founded to gather support for Iranian human rights activists and defenders who are advocating for their civil, political, social, and economic rights within the framework of international treaties and standards that define Iran's obligations. The campaign documents Iran's compliance with its international human rights obligations and publicizes this information to help advance human rights and social movements in Iran. The website contains a press archive, a blog, and a library with a multitude of reports and information on various topics.

United States Institute of Peace
1200 Seventeenth St. NW, Washington, DC   20036
(202) 457-1700 • fax: (202) 429-6063
website: www.usip.org

The US Institute of Peace is an independent, nonpartisan, national institution established and funded by Congress. Its goals are to help prevent and resolve violent international conflicts, promote postconflict stability and development, and increase conflict management capacity, tools, and intellectual capital worldwide. The website contains an online book called *The Iran Primer*, which includes information about Iran contributed by fifty of the world's top scholars on Iran, representing some twenty foreign policy think tanks, eight universities, and senior foreign policy officials from six US administrations. The book provides overviews of Iran's politics, economy, military, foreign policy, and nuclear programs; discusses US policies toward Iran; and offers commentary on recent developments in Iran and US-Iran relations.

Bibliography

Books

Tawfiq Alsaif	*Islamic Democracy and Its Limits: The Iranian Experience Since 1979.* London, UK: Saqi Books 2008.
Said Amir Arjomand	*After Khomeini: Iran Under His Successors.* New York: Oxford University Press, 2009.
Fakhreddin Azimi	*Iran: The Crisis of Democracy: From the Exile of Reza Shah to the Fall of Musaddiq.* London, UK: I.B. Tauris, 2009.
Fakhreddin Azimi	*The Quest for Democracy in Iran: A Century of Struggle Against Authoritarian Rule.* Cambridge, MA: Harvard University Press, 2010.
Hamid Dabashi	*Iran, the Green Movement and the USA: The Fox and the Paradox.* London, UK: Zed Books, 2010.
Akbar Ganji, Joshua Cohen, and Abbas Milani	*The Road to Democracy in Iran.* Cambridge, MA: MIT Press, 2008.
Ali Gheissari and Vali Nasr	*Democracy in Iran: History and the Quest for Liberty.* New York: Oxford University Press, 2009.
Nader Hashemi and Danny Postel	*The People Reloaded: The Green Movement and the Struggle for Iran's Future.* Brooklyn, NY: Melville House, 2011.

Hooman Majd   *The Ayatollah Begs to Differ: The Paradox of Modern Iran.* New York: Anchor Books, 2009.

Hooman Majd   *The Ayatollahs' Democracy: An Iranian Challenge.* New York: Norton, 2010.

Ali Mirsepassi   *Democracy in Modern Iran: Islam, Culture, and Political Change.* New York: New York University Press, 2010.

Azadeh Moaveni   *Honeymoon in Tehran: Two Years of Love and Danger in Iran.* New York: Random House, 2010.

Scott Peterson   *Let the Swords Encircle Me: Iran—A Journey Behind the Headlines.* New York: Simon & Schuster, 2010.

Barbara Slavin   *Bitter Friends, Bosom Enemies: Iran, the U.S., and the Twisted Path to Confrontation.* New York: St. Martin's, 2009.

Amir Taheri   *The Persian Night: Iran Under the Khomeinist Revolution.* New York: Encounter Books, 2010.

Robin Wright   *The Iran Primer: Power, Politics, and U.S. Policy.* Washington, DC: United States Institute of Peace Press, 2010.

Periodicals and Internet Sources

Abolhassan Bani-Sadr	"Will Democratic Movements in Tunisia and Egypt Heed Lessons of Iran's Revolution?" *Christian Science Monitor*, January 28, 2011. www.csmonitor.com.
Saeed Kamali Dehghan	"Iran Protests See Reinvigorated Activists Take to the Streets in Thousands," *Guardian* (UK), February 14, 2011. www.guardian.co.uk.
Elizabeth Dovell	"Political Salon: Human Rights in Iran," *World Policy Blog*, November 29, 2010. www.worldpolicy.org.
Golnaz Esfandiari	"The Twitter Devolution," *Foreign Policy*, June 7, 2010. www.foreignpolicy.com.
Mehrun Etebari	"How Tehran Sees Tunis: From Iran, It's More About 1979 than 2009," *Foreign Policy*, January 28, 2011. www.foreignpolicy.com.
Foreign Policy	"Misreading Tehran: Leading Iranian-American Writers Revisit a Year of Dreams and Discouragement," June 7, 2010. www.foreignpolicy.com.
Christopher Helman	"Oil Giants Fear Revolution Is Coming to Them Next," *Forbes*, February 2, 2011. http://blogs.forbes.com/.

Mohammed Khan "A Tale of Two Protests: The Subdued US Reaction to Events in Egypt Sits in Sharp Contrast to Its Previous Support for Iranian Protesters," Aljazeera, February 1, 2011. http://english.aljazeera.net.

Edith M. Lederer and John Daniszewski "Ahmadinejad: The Future Is Iran's," Associated Press, September 20, 2010. www.washingtontimes.com.

Miranda Leitsinger "Will Egypt Re-energize Iran's 'Green Movement'?" MSNBC.com, February 14, 2011. www.msnbc.msn.com.

Flynt Leverett and Hillary Mann Leverett "Ahmadinejad Won. Get Over It," Politico, June 15, 2009. http://dyn.politico.com.

Hooman Majd "The Beginning of the End: The New Demonstrations in Tehran Suggest the Street Protests Will Fail," Newsweek, July 13, 2009. www.newsweek.com.

Hooman Majd "The Great Revolution That Wasn't," Newsweek, June 10, 2010. www.newsweek.com.

Ryan Mauro "The Green Revolution Isn't Over," Frontpagemag.com, June 16, 2010. http://frontpagemag.com.

Abbas Milani "Iran: A Coup in Three Steps: The Road to 2009's Velvet Green Revolution," Defining Ideas, June 15, 2009. www.hoover.org.

The National	"Iran: A Silenced Revolution," August 13, 2010. www.thenational.ae.
Jason Rezaian	"What Went Wrong? Why Did Iran's Pro-democracy Movement Stall?" *Slate*, June 10, 2010. www.slate.com.
Laura Secor	"Interview: Mehdi Karroubi on Iran's Green Movement," *New Yorker*, October 12, 2010. www.newyorker.com/online/.
Simon Tisdall	"Egypt Revolt Has Iran in a Spin," *Guardian* (UK), February 1, 2011. www.guardian.co.uk.
William Yong	"Iran Sees Rise of Islamic Hard-Liners," *New York Times*, January 28, 2011. www.nytimes.com.

Index